D1499047

april 1987

ENGLISH LITERATURE

Opening Up the Canon

English Literature

OPENING UP THE CANON

 *Selected Papers
from the English Institute, 1979*

New Series, no. 4

Edited by Leslie A. Fiedler and Houston A. Baker, Jr.

THE JOHNS HOPKINS UNIVERSITY PRESS
BALTIMORE AND LONDON

The Johns Hopkins University Press, Baltimore, Maryland 21218
The Johns Hopkins Press Ltd., London

Library of Congress Cataloging in Publication Data

English Institute.
    English literature.

    (Selected papers from the English Institute ;
1979, new ser., no. 4)
    1. English literature—20th century—History and
criticism—Congresses. 2. English language in
foreign countries—Congresses. 3. Literature and
society—Congresses. I. Fiedler, Leslie A.
II. Baker, Houston A. III. Title. IV. Series:
English Institute. Selected papers from the
English Institute ; new ser., no. 4
PR9080.E53 1981   820'.9   80-8863
ISBN 0-8018-2591-1

Contents

Preface

The present collection of essays represents an attempt to escape from the parochialism that ordinarily limits discussions at meetings of the English Institute. It represents, in fact, *two* attempts, separately conceived and planned, which somehow worked together, turning out to have, if not a common goal, at least a shared discontent with the present situation.

The authors of the pieces in this collection under the heading of "English as a World Language for Literature" sometimes found themselves in disagreement with those included under the heading "The Institution of Literature." Yet, in retrospect, it seems as if they shared a common cause.

Not only do the pieces in both categories deal with subjects not ordinarily treated at sessions of the English Institute—being more political, more polemical, more passionate—but their mode of presentation is different as well. Many of them, that is to say, are informal, colloquial, confessional, while others are anecdotal or allegorical—one of them, shamelessly, a short story. It is doubtless misleading, moreover, to speak of them as essays; some at least were designed to be heard rather than read, and consequently what appears on the printed page misrepresents their original impact and intent.

We considered for a while, in fact, releasing this volume along with a tape of the proceedings, but technical difficulties deterred us. At some points in the pages that follow, therefore, readers will have to imagine the music of the discourse, quite as if they held in their hands a libretto or a score.

Lacking, too, is the controversy that surrounded many of these addresses: the protests, demurrers, and often hostile questions from the floor. But this, too, should be easily imagined by readers who, doubtless, will have objections of their own to the style or content of one essay or another.

The contributions to this volume, individually or collectively, raise critical questions about the study of literature in the university, limited as it is by unconscious assumptions of the teachers, rooted in race, class, and gender. Merely to recognize the problem is to begin solving it.

LESLIE A. FIEDLER

Introduction

ENGLISH AS A WORLD LANGUAGE FOR LITERATURE
A SESSION FOR THE 1979 ENGLISH INSTITUTE

 There are a number of issues that might be considered in this session of the English Institute. If one begins with the notion that literature is a representation of experience, one must ask how it is possible to represent in the English language experiences that occur, so to speak, in other languages. Philosophers of language assert that we do not think a thought and then transform the thought into language. Instead our thoughts are inseparable from the languages that give them form. How, then, does Tewa or Yoruba or Sotho thought achieve literary form in English? How, given the inseparability of thought and language, and the diversity of the world's language communities, should one approach the notion that English has global status as a literary language? What presuppositions are embodied in this view, and what are the implications?

Obviously, the conception of English as a "world language" is rooted in Western economic history. World trade, investment capitalism, and a market economy were predicated on fundamental revisions of feudal definitions of *Homo laborans* (man as laborer). The channel of communication for world trade was likely to be the language containing the most fitting statement of these revised definitions. Portuguese, Dutch, German, French, and English have all served as channels during the past three and a half centuries. The global ascendency of English as a trade language, as a system giving semantic force to technological views of man and nature, has conditioned the study and evaluation of the English language. English, that is to say, seems a fitting language in which to think about modern man.

It was this proposition, or one very similar to it, that led Richard Wright to say in *Black Boy* that his attainment of "Prospero's" language separated him forever from the peasant world of his father. Looking at the gnarled hands and the primitive agricultural tools of his aged parent, Wright reflects that he himself has been lifted in the arms of Western experience (i.e., English as a language for modern literature and thought) and carried to exalted heights. A subtle resonance is created in the autobiography between this passage at the end of the first chapter and the concluding incident of chapter two, in which a black man points to the heavens and says to the protagonist: "Boy, remember this. You're seeing man fly." The point here, of course, is that Wright seems to feel that thinking about contemporary man and culture is inseparably linked to thinking in the "standard literary English" of industrial societies. One studies the language and grants a positive evaluation to it because to do so is to encounter a range of experience that is otherwise inaccessible.

This, I think, is also what some neocolonial scholars, writers, and economic advisers are suggesting when they say that they cannot express their "most complex and striking notions" in any language other than English. (A Yale University professor from a formerly colonized portion of the world once expressed this point of view to me with all the furious energy of a convert to a new faith. My response at the time, some three years ago, must have left him feeling that I was being stubborn, coy, or obtuse. I suggested that the Creole of his native island might be quite suitable for "advanced thought.")

To adopt an explanation grounded in economics alone, however, is to drastically reduce the scope of an inquiry into English as a world language for literature. Judged exclusively on the basis of its force in the economic arena, English clearly has (for the moment) a hands-down advantage. If one introduces the

conceptualization of man as *Homo ludens* (man at play), however, what happens to the indisputable economic authority of
English? If one extends the range of the modern experience to
include modes of behavior that are not traditionally defined as
essential to processes of economic production and distribution,
does English then drop in the scale of value? In the factory
hospital episode of Ralph Ellison's *Invisible Man,* the protagonist's discovery of his basic humanity seems to occur in an
environment where spoken language fails to operate in the
accustomed way. He falls into a reverie of the agrarian South in
which the prominent images are of black convicts fleeing the
enforced labor of the chain gang, of a black trumpeter playing
a sacred song called "The Heavenly City," and of his elderly
grandmother reciting to him a folk rhyme whose cosmology
begins with God in heaven engaged in a ludic act of creation.
His return from this reverie is marked by silence; he cannot
hear the words that the representatives of industrial society seem
to be directing toward him. Their lips move in soundless pan-
tomime. The protagonist is baffled by the inability of those
who wish to be his captors to communicate with him. "But we
are all human," he thinks to himself. What this thought and,
indeed, the episode as a whole seem to imply is: "Yes, we are
all human, but *their* language, since it is centered on *Homo
laborans,* too severely discounts realms of experience that are
fundamental to the notion of a human being." Call it the ludic
dimension, the marginal zone, or the liminal region, the protagonist seems to suggest, but give due recognition to *Homo
ludens* in any contemporary definition of the term "human."

I do not want to insist here that these two neatly self-
contained conceptualizations of human beings—economic man
defined by the English language, and man at play, defined by a
kind of wordless dreaminess—confront each other across a great
divide. Instead, my concern is to place in proper perspective
the economic ascendancy of English and the historical correla-
tion between this ascendancy and processes of modern thought.

In a sense, I want to go back to those pre-English-speaking moments in the life of world societies and to trace the complex interactions in thought and action between the worlds of the Tewa, the Yoruba, and the Sotho, up to the point where, say, a Yoruba speaker makes the decision that English is indeed a world language for literature and begins to use English for his own acts of creative, linguistic expression designed for a reading public. I suspect that by the time the Yoruba writer makes such a decision, his knowledge of English includes the rules and relationships, signs and codes, that make the language suitable for his expressive designs. The world of *Homo ludens,* crafted in a non-English-speaking society, has come into the purview of English as a result of acculturative interaction between the Yoruba writer and the English-language trader. Notions of *Homo laborans* that modify forever the trader's ethnocentric ideas of economic production and distribution have also come into the purview of English.

Writing of the Bandung Conference, which took place in Indonesia in 1956, and which gave birth to the concept of a "Third World," Richard Wright asserts in *The Color Curtain* that one result of the conference, and indeed a necessary correlative of the rise of a Third World that employed English as a lingua franca, was the introduction of a new "moral dimension" into the English language. I believe that what Wright intended by his statement was that acculturation is a two-way process. Those whose labor and resources are exploited, whose land is annexed and possessed, whose language and culture are derogated by the colonizer are, nevertheless, vibrant human beings who have a profound effect on those who come in the name of civilization. Not only do the colonized or the enslaved populations preserve vital elements of their indigenous cultural styles during the ordeal of their servitude, but they also modify the basic cultural grammar of the colonizer. Conrad's Mr. Kurtz discovers the truth of this assertion at the cost of his life.

To simply say that English rules the economic heartland and

thus controls the literary world is to foreclose far-ranging inquiry. The fact that a Sotho writer claims that he has chosen English because it guarantees a wide audience and ensures access to the literary reproduction systems of a world market may be less important as a literary consideration than what the writer has actually made of the English language as a literary agency. One might want to ask, for example, what summits of experience inaccessible to occupants of the heartland have been incorporated into the world of English literature? What literary strategies have been employed by the Sotho writer to preserve and communicate culturally-specific meanings? What codes of analysis and evaluation must be articulated in order to render accurate explanations for a Sotho or a Tewa or a Yoruba literary work written in English?

I am quite ready to assert that English as a world language for literature achieves this status through the actions of the world at large, and not through the actions of, as it were, *The English*. I am further prepared to suggest that those who are within the traditional, economically-sanctioned territories of English literary expression are often incapable of comprehending what men and women in the world-at-large have made of English. The realms of experience represented in the language today, and the literary-critical and theoretical strategies that must be employed in order to grasp them, are subjects that seem to be almost exclusive possessions of a Third World. The Third World is, of course, a region comparable to Blake's realm of the fourfold vision, that is, a difficult region to negotiate if the mind and the mind's eye are not fully open.

HOUSTON A. BAKER, JR.

Dennis Brutus

English and the Dynamics
of South African Creative Writing

My discussion of the predicament of the creative writer in South Africa is essentially an examination of the context in which that writer operates and the factors at work on him or her—particularly those that inhibit creative work.

"The influences that operate on the creative writer" would more exactly describe what I am trying to do. Because South Africa is a strange society—in the sense of peculiar—it is helpful to look at the forces in the society that function either to promote or to inhibit creative writing. To do this, however, is to look also at the society and indeed briefly to sketch the development of writing in English in South Africa.

South Africa is currently independent, and began its existence, in European history, anyway, first as a Dutch, and then as a British colony. Writing in English in South Africa began in 1854 with Thomas Pringle, who was one of the settlers brought to South Africa in a large contingent at the end of the Napoleonic War. Pringle brought with him something of the English liberal tradition to the extent that within four years he was being forced out, forced back to Britain because of his criticism of the colonial administration. That exercise of power by an autocratic governor is, perhaps, as good a note as any on which to begin the history of English literature in South Africa. Since then, a few figures have won some international recognition. They include Alan Paton; Nadine Gordimer, probably South Africa's most distinguished novelist; and Athol Fugard, who has achieved an international reputation as a playwright. Before that we had a few rather less well-known names on the international scene: Olive Schreiner, with her novel *The Story of an African Farm,* and William Plomer, whose precocious novel *Turbott Wolfe* was written when he was only nineteen. For those of us who follow black writing in Africa, there are also those names that are known all over the world in terms of black literature, such as Alex LaGuma; Mazisi Kunene, who writes in Zulu; Peter Abrahams, long exiled from South Africa; and Ezekiel Mphahlele.

The white South African writers, who enjoy advantages in publication and facilities and contacts not known to blacks, tend to be better known. South African society consists of two principal colonial streams: the English settlers and the Dutch settlers. The latter developed their own form of Dutch, called Afrikaans, a kind of patois that derived from it and is less well known. The Afrikaners have a much narrower audience. One of them, the poet, Breyten Breytenbach, has achieved some degree of international recognition. This recognition may, however, be the consequence of his antigovernment activities. He is currently serving a nine-year prison sentence in South Africa, and this, rather than his distinction in poetry, may be the basis of his reputation.

It is useful to look at some of the salient features of the South African context of society as they affect the writer. Following is some fairly crude information: roughly 25,000 books have been banned in South Africa and declared illegal. Possession of these books, reading them, and quoting from them are all criminal acts. Some fairly obvious books, such as obscene publications, are banned on the grounds of pornography. But many of the banned books would be considered harmless, if perhaps radical, elsewhere in the world. As of now 750 persons in South Africa are banned from publishing in South Africa or from having their work read or quoted in South Africa. They are also forbidden to attend any gathering where more than two people are present. (I myself fell into all of these categories when I was living in South Africa, and my work continues to be banned.) Most of the major writers, both white and black, are in exile at the present time. And perhaps a more dismaying statistic is that at least three major Afrikaner poets, and twice as many black writers according to some reports, committed suicide in South Africa in recent years.

Toby Moyana, in a lengthy essay titled "Problems of the Creative Writer in South Africa," contended that the government was literally legislating literature out of existence, that it was becoming impossible for people to write. It might be worthwhile to mention some of the legislation. One of the blanket laws that permits much of control legislation dates back to 1927; it is called the Bantu Administration Act. Since then the South African government has passed the Entertainment Censorship Act of 1931, the Unlawful Organization Act (1960), and the Publications and Entertainment Act (1956). In 1969 a great kind of umbrella law that makes virtually everything illegal if the state *deems* it to be illegal, called the General Laws Amendment Act, was passed.

The mechanism by which these laws operate is instructive. Since about 1963 South Africa has had a Publications Control Board; this board determines what is fit for publication. It creates a real problem for publishers because the banning decisions often take place only after publication—after the publishers have already committed themselves to production. When the book is about to go on sale, the government issues a ruling that the publication is illegal, and this can cause great financial hardship.

It is sometimes said that repression may stimulate activity and that therefore there is a kind of paradoxical merit in being put under the pressures that are placed on South African writers. Oddly enough, there may be some evidence that confirms this theory in the society. It is true, for instance, that in 1976 when there was a massive uprising in the ghettos, especially those in the South West Townships that are lumped together under the word "Soweto," there was an incredible efflorescence of writing in the ghetto—particularly of poetry. Even more exciting has been the appearance of a kind of improvised theatre, an open air or guerrilla theatre with improvised poetry, much of which is not committed to paper. The poets seem especially to be responsive to the new tensions, the new pressures that are developing in the society.

It should be said the blacks in the ghettos see the affluence and the wealth of the apartheid society as being directly dependent on the sustenance it receives from outside countries, particularly Western countries. The massive injections of capital, and the transfer of technology to the apartheid society, are seen very clearly in the ghettos as factors that enable a minority regime to remain in power. Perhaps the greatest support that the West has given to South Africa (there is little more that they can give in addition to this) has been to provide South Africa with the capability of manufacturing nuclear weapons. This has been achieved through the assistance of the United States, France, and West Germany. It seems there is not much more that can be done except to continue as before. Many blacks feel that the West has made its ultimate commitment to the white society, and this commitment extends even into the realm of the arts. In literature, in the theatre, in ballet, and in music, the racist and repressive South African society continues to draw sustenance from the West. The blacks see this as simply one more dimension of Western support for a racist minority.

I should add at this point that very soon the United Nations will be launching new initiatives aimed at an embargo of South Africa; this will include a cultural embargo. There are people in the United States who could, I believe, make a significant contribution by supporting a cultural embargo.

How have the blacks responded in South Africa? How has creativity been expressed in this repressive society? And how would one answer the question raised by Houston Baker about the new insights that are brought into the English language by writers whose first language is not English? We may have a different world view and a different cosmology. I spent some time pondering this and came up with what may be a disappointing reply: I cannot see a great deal that is significantly new or inventive. If there were time, I could catalogue some of the minor variations, particularly in African perception of a creator, a universal force that tends generally to be female. I could tell you that the African sense of time is circular, and that the living and the dead coexist in the same kind of human fabric. I think these are incipient rather than developed features. They are implicit in some of the writings and, given an opportunity, may become more evident. There may, in fact, be an explanation for the failure to come up with new perceptions through communication in English. We are dealing with a society where communication between people is illegal, a society that creates a battery of laws that makes communication between people from different cultures or from different groups a criminal act. It can be a crime in South Africa for two people of different races to drink tea together, or to be in the same restaurant together.

One example, my favorite, is drawn from the area in which I was most deeply involved in South Africa—that of sport. A black athlete running on the same track with a white athlete could be arrested, or a black tennis player on the same tennis court with a white tennis player could go to prison. There are very blatant forms of discrimination imposed by the legal system, for which there are sanctions. Those who attempt to communicate are punished. It may be that in such a society one can neither come up with insights and perceptions into another culture nor with new ways of expressing what already exists in that culture.

The substance of the writing, particularly the new poetry, is first of all an attempt to articulate a community experience, to convey what is in the society rather than in the individual. Of course, in the African artistic and literary traditions, especially in the oral tradition, there is so much that antecedes the expression of ideas and the feelings of the community as opposed to the feelings of the individual. We have currently a completely new batch of young poets coming out of the ghettos, and their themes are pretty much the same: anger at the cruelty and the injustice of the system, and an attempt to articulate that anger, to go beyond it, and to function as rallying points, as interpreters of the feeling of the society. The titles of the works are revealing. One of the most important, banned almost immediately after publication, is called *Cry Rage*; it was a joint venture by James Matthews and Gladys Thomas. Another, published shortly thereafter with the work of nine poets in it, was banned immediately—that was called *Black Voices Shout.* In addition to books, magazines, many of them ephemeral, are also banned; some of them are banned by issue rather than by a blanket ban. A magazine like *Staffrider,* which is a vehicle for black writers, had its first issue banned, but the second, third, and fourth issues are still available. Perhaps it, too, will cease publication, as many of the others have. The writing is now published mainly in magazines and periodicals; these are often joint ventures by whites and blacks who are opponents of the system. Books of this kind have become rare.

It is important to remember, I think, that because of the colonial history of South Africa, every educated black is exposed to the mainstream of the English literary tradition. Blacks begin learning Shakespeare and Wordsworth in junior school ("Daffodils" is learned in almost every school). In high school blacks begin to read what might be called classics: Dickens's *A Tale of Two Cities* and Cooper's *The Last of the Mohicans* are included in high school reading. They might even read an early Shakespeare comedy. By the time one goes to university, one is exposed to three years of English. If you are going to major in it, you go through the traditional kind of syllabus, beginning with Chaucer, through the Elizabethans (and perhaps the Metaphysicals), on to the Romantics and the Victorians, and perhaps reading a few of the modern poets as well. This pretty much is the range of exposure for an African being educated under a system inherited from the British university system. The example of the commitment by English writers, and the criticisms of society by such writers as Milton, Wordsworth, Blake, and Shelley, strike responsive chords in the African writer. Indeed, some African writers have been criticized for a too-slavish imitation of their English models.

The break, it is evident, comes in the very recent past; it is a move away from traditional form toward a very conscious attempt at immediacy, at direct and unadorned communication. This, I fear, would suffer if it were judged by any academic canon, for it hardly conforms to accepted notions about the craft of poetry. They would reply, quite frankly, that they are not interested in creating works that will endure, that they are not interested in creating works that will pass muster in the university; they would say instead that their preoccupation is with immediate and effective communication with the people around them. That may be not an unworthy goal.

The writer suffers, however, not only from the restraints and limitations imposed on him by the legal system, but by a whole new set of pressures that flow from convention and prejudice rather than from the law. These restraints, these pressures on black writers and writing are due to the arrogance of the literary critics and the contemptuous handling of black writers by established literary persons. It seems to me to be so pervasive that I am beginning to wonder whether arrogance is not an occupational hazard for all critics. Of course, I ought to give some examples of this, and I offer something that is of fairly recent vintage and this is typical. The South African critic A. G. Wyett, who has taught English literature in Kenya, Rhodesia, and Swaziland before coming to South Africa (those were his credentials), discusses the dilemma of black South African poetry in an essay. He says the black poet has to determine how he is going to make meaningful use of a centuries-old, culturally-enriched language in the relatively undeveloped cultural environment in which he finds himself. He finds that the black poet often falls into the trap of pretentiousness, writing flat and

clichéd lines, while believing that his lines are really successful
poetic creations. Wyett does, however, balance this comment
with something else, which may be a redeeming comment (I
don't know, because what he concedes is the following): "The
poet may create some remote possible line, but this achievement may be attained more by chance, by fortuitous ignorance
of style, idiom, imitation and so on, rather than by deliberate
artistic intention. For one thing, the black writer has to remember that the part chance plays in the creation of poetry in
a language belonging to a foreign culture has yet to be explored.
Perhaps we ought to hold off until exploration is complete."
Perhaps Wyett himself would undertake to be a trailblazer. Wyett goes on to say that the evidence may yet be found to support his belief that good lines written by the black poet in a
language not his own are the product of accident, rather than
choice.

We return to our critic Wyett, who says: "If poets recognize
Wyett goes on to criticize African poetry for another weak-
ness: the poet has become too committed, too much of an engaged poet. Here Wyett can cite W. H. Auden's authority;
Auden said (and I think that this has become, unfortunately,
almost an article of faith), "Let a poet if he wants to, write engaged poems. But let him remember this: the only person who
will benefit from it is himself. The evil or injustice will remain
exactly as it would have been if he had kept his mouth shut."
I think Auden underestimates his impact on his own, and on
future, generations. I believe he *has* moved others through his
sense of concern for humanity. So, he may have judged his own
work too meanly.

We return to our critic Wyett, who says: "If poets recognize
the enormously healthy potential open to them in a poetic rebellion, they will eventually create notorious poems. At present
the prevalent critical emphasis on the sterile and toxic impotence of resentment is engendering a poetry characterized by
immaturity." Now you can see paternalism beginning to show
its ugly head. For he goes on: "Yet we must not be too severe in

our condemnation of it, just as we should not always be severe on the young. And there by the same token, we must not be unduly indulgent, otherwise the healthy young tradition may well grow warped or stunted."

There is a great deal more of that kind of reasoning, but I am inclined to pass over it. I wish, however (to balance that), to quote a correspondent who wrote to the journal *Contrast* protesting the condescending and arrogant attitudes of critics. H. Davis says that the insensitivity and incompetence of Wyett is underlined by his admitted failure to grasp the meaning of a poem that he quotes. Perhaps Davis might have been left in possession of the field, but the editor of the journal (and *Contrast* is a fairly authoritative journal by South African literary standards) comes to the defense of the journal: "I think it is correct to say that no member of this magazine's editorial board has ever looked back or judged for acceptance a manuscript of a poem or any other work in the light of the race or skin color of the contributor. It therefore comes as news to me that ten or a dozen or whatever number of black poems have been published in our pages. Good for the poets. If these poets are black Africans writing in English, which is not their mother tongue, then their achievement is all the more impressive." Davis goes on to say, "Since this periodical first appeared in December 1960, and they have had ten or twelve blacks since 1960, it has stuck to the original concept of the founding group that its policy is to have *no policy*."

"Of course, it can be asserted that *no politics* is also politics, and that in the South African context, it is well nigh impossible to open one's mouth or to take up a pen without being committed to a political act." Having made that statement, the editor makes no effort to rebut it, a situation that I found curious, to say the least.

In order to take the issue just a little further afield—or perhaps to bring it a little nearer home—I am going to refer to another critical aberration, but not one that is limited to South

Africa. Chinua Achebe, the distinguished African novelist, gave
an address at a welcome reception, which was given for us by
the mayor of Berlin, at a festival intended to open dialogue between Africa and West Germany, or indeed, between Africa and
the West. In the course of responding to the welcome, Achebe
made the remark that Africans are interested in dialogue on the
basis of equality, that they are *not* interested in the kind of
partnership that is that of a rider and a horse. Achebe talked
about Joseph Conrad and expressed alarm at the determination
of the West to have Africa explained to it by Western experts,
and at the way the West very deliberately excludes Africans,
who themselves are attempting to interpret their culture and
their country. He says that Europe's (and America's) reliance
on its own experts in reporting on the true nature of Africa
would not worry anybody if it did not, at the same time, attempt to exclude the testimony of Africans. But it often does.
He quotes an expert who says that "the real African" lives in
the bush, goes around naked, and tells fairy stories about the
crocodile and the elephant; and he adds wryly, "As the pace of
change quickens, there won't be many authentic Africans
left around. Certainly not any with the wholesome and unques-
tioning admiration of white people, which was the chief attraction of the bush African. In any case, the businessman who
is in Africa for profit today isn't going to consult a witch doctor
for his opinion on an investment first."

He then brings it even nearer home. He discusses a recent article in the *New York Times Book Review.* Elizabeth Hardwick
interviewed V. S. Naipaul on the publication of his new book, *A
Bend in the River.* Hardwick commented: "Naipual's work is a
creative reflection upon a devastating lack of historical prepara-
tion, upon the anguish of whole countries when peoples are able
to quote." She quotes, according to Achebe, with apparent glee
and approval from the growing corpus of scornful work which
Naipaul has written on Africa, India, and South America and
from his report on his Congo travels, where he sees ". . . native

people camping on the ruins of civilization" and "the bush creeming back as you stood there." This is Achebe's comment: "Reading Elizabeth Hardwick's interview, an absurd or rather pathetic picture rises from the printed page. An old American lady lapping up like a wide-eyed little girl every drop of pretentious drivel that falls from the lips of a literary guru who is smart enough to fill his devotee with comforting myths." Her last question, predictably, was "What is the future of Africa?" His part and equally predictable reply was: "Africa *has* no future." This new Conrad figure, says Achebe, neither European nor African, will have his day and pass on, leaving the problem of dialogue, which has plagued Afro-American European relations for centuries, unsolved until Europe is ready to concede total African humanity.

Again, let me redress the balance just for a moment by pointing to some very distinguished American critics who have written with perception and sympathy on African literature. Perhaps it is invidious to single out particular pieces that I found especially valuable, but I do wish to mention Wilfred Cartey's book, *Whispers From a Continent,* and Paul Theroux's excellent early essay, "Voices from the Skull," on poetry in Africa.

As we leave the seventies and enter the eighties, I think it might be helpful to attempt a prediction about the literature being produced by English-speaking white South Africans and the English-speaking black South Africans. We might also look at those who are writing in Afrikaans, the other official language. There is, of course, an enormous body of material being turned out in the African languages themselves: Zulu, Xosa, Sotho, and others. Some of it is oral, some of it is improvised and passed on. Some of it is committed to paper. There is a very special bind here, though, that I ought to explain. Because the apartheid government—the minority white government—has tried to revive the old tribal structures and to force the Africans back into those structures in order to prevent them from participating in the present political processes, the Africans tend to be suspicious even of their own languages and literary vehicles. They are fearful that these might be turned against them and used as one further pretext to force them back into a tribal mode within a broad policy of what are known as the Bantustans—a strategy that is aimed at forcing black Africans back into tribal structures. But nevertheless there is a great deal of literature being created. The English writers, I fear, will probably go on like Wyett and the editor of *Contrast*: not only arrogant but blind—or blinkered to their own arrogance. It may well be said that South Africa is not the only part of the world where a certain arrogance is exhibited toward minority writers.

The Afrikaners have an interesting opportunity, because as of now, political power is vested in the hands of the Afrikaans-speaking minority (although they hold their power with the collaboration of the English-speaking group). It may be that if the Afrikaners can reach their own people and persuade them that the issue is not survival, as they contend, but rather the question of the surrender of privilege, they can perform an extremely useful function in the society and actually help to change the direction of its history, which seems now headed for inevitable disaster.

It seems to me that the black African writers can only become more defiant and intransigent; that they will continue to be, as they have been in the past, rallying centers around which groups form in opposition in their resistance to the system. Nadine Gordimer, in an extremely penetrating essay on the myths in the literature of South Africa, has pointed to two myths that seem to help in understanding the white literature. She finds, particularly among the Afrikaans writers, a tendency to blame the British imperial power which crushed them at the beginning of the century, to blame that power for the ills of the present, and to say, "We ourselves were rolled over by the British imperial Juggernaut. We cannot take responsibility for what is wrong in society as of now."

The other myth, which is fairly closely related to it, is that more and more (and a specific example is a quite brilliant work called *Dustlands* in English), by an examination of the behavior of other societies, particularly the killings in Vietnam, or genocidal activities in New Zealand, Tasmania, or Australia, or among the American Indians in this country, parallels can be found for the behavior of the South African regime, which enables them to say, "We're as bad as everybody else, but no worse." Therefore they can continue doing what they are doing now.

Gordimer suggests that these are two of the most important myths that enable white South Africans to live comfortably with themselves. I suggest that the one that will emerge more strongly is the argument that white South Africans can deny black South Africans political rights, and indeed even South African nationality, by offering them instead some kind of dummy citizenship in a little client or satellite state, carved off from South Africa as the country is dismembered by the process called the Bantustan Policy. They will then be able to argue, "We have not really denied them rights; we have simply substituted other rights for those we have deprived them of."

In this context, the process of creative writing for both white South Africa and black South Africa becomes much more difficult. You have the battery of laws to contend with; you have the prejudices in the society; you have the myths that justify continued oppression in the society. You have, unfortunately, the money still being pipelined into South Africa from outside to keep the regime solvent and, indeed, prosperous. And so we roll on to an agonizing and inevitable destructiveness.

I would like to close by harking back to a point I made earlier: it may be that those of us who have a concern about creative writing, about creativity, and beyond that, about the simple business of being human—that all of us can be involved in the process that reduces the aid currently being given to the South African regime. By doing what we already do a great deal more, we can actually minimize the area, the extent, the duration, and the scale of the conflict that must come to South Africa, and in that way we can make our own humane contribution.

Edward Kamau Brathwaite

English in the Caribbean

NOTES ON NATION LANGUAGE AND POETRY
AN ELECTRONIC LECTURE*

You may excel
in knowledge of their tongue
and universal ties may bind you close to them;
but what they say, and how they feel—
the subtler details of their meaning,
thinking, feeling, reaching—
these are closed to you and me . . .
as are, indeed, the interleaves of speech
—our speech—which fall to them . . .

> dead leaves . . .

> —G. Adali-Morty, "Belonging" from *Messages*

The Negro in the West Indies becomes proportionately whiter—that is,
he becomes closer to being a real human being—in direct ratio to his
mastery of the language.

> —Frantz Fanon, *Peau noire, masque blancs*

Yurokon held the twine in his hands as if with a snap, a single fierce
pull, he would break it *now* at last. Break the land. Break the sea. Break
the savannah. Break the forest. Break the twig. Break the bough.

> —Wilson Harris, *Sleepers of Roraima*

What I am going to talk about this morning is language
from the Caribbean, the process of using English in a different
way from the "norm." English in a sense as I prefer to call

---

*Professor Brathwaite says of nation language that, "When it is written, you lose
the sound or the noise, and therefore you lose part of the meaning." Surely this
written representation of Professor Brathwaite's unscripted remarks, which I have
edited, loses some of the magnificent force and meaning that his live performance
conveyed in Cambridge. The reader, for example, will not only miss the sound of
Professor Brathwaite's voice but also the sound of the taped recordings and accom-
panying music that added much to his presentation. Nonetheless, the following remarks are in themselves quite remarkable in what they convey of a new sense of
sound, and noise, emerging from the present-day Caribbean.—H.A.B.†

†Professor Baker's sensitive version has been further revised by the speaker, who
has added footnotes and some texts.

15

it. English in an ancient sense. English in a very traditional
sense. And sometimes not English at all, but language.

I start my thoughts, taking up from the discussion developed
after Dennis Brutus's excellent presentation. Without logic,
and through instinct, the people who spoke with Dennis from
the floor yesterday brought up the question of language. Actually, Dennis's presentation had nothing to do with language.
He was speaking about the structural condition of South Africa. But instinctively people recognized that the structural
condition described by Dennis had very much to do with language. He didn't concentrate on the language aspect of it because there wasn't enough time and because it was not his main
concern. But it was interesting that your instincts, not your
logic, moved you toward the question of the relationship between language and culture, language and structure. In his
case, it was English, and English as spoken by Africans, and
the native languages as spoken by Africans.

We in the Caribbean have a similar kind of plurality. We have
English, which is the imposed language on much of the archi-
pelago; it is an imperial language, as are French, Dutch, and
Spanish. We also have what we call Creole English, which is a
mixture of English and an adaptation that English took in the
new environment of the Caribbean when it became mixed with
the other imported languages. We have also what is called *nation language,* which is the kind of English spoken by the people who were brought to the Caribbean, not the official English
now, but the language of slaves and laborers—the servants who
were brought in by the conquistadors. Finally, we have the rem-
nants of ancestral languages still persisting in the Caribbean.
There is Amerindian, which is active in certain parts of Central
America but not in the Caribbean because the Amerindians are
a destroyed people, and their languages were practically destroyed. We have Hindi, spoken by some of the more traditional
East Indians who live in the Caribbean, and there are also varie-
ties of Chinese.[1] And, miraculously, there are survivals of Afri-

can languages still persisting in the Caribbean. So we have that spectrum—that prism—of languages similar to the kind of structure that Dennis described for South Africa. Now, I have to give you some kind of background to the development of these languages, the historical development of this plurality, because I can't take it for granted that you know and understand the history of the Caribbean.

The Caribbean is a set of islands stretching out from Florida in a mighty curve. You must know of the Caribbean at least from television, at least now with hurricane David* coming right into it. The islands stretch out in an arc of some two thousand miles from Florida through the Atlantic to the South American coast, and they were originally inhabited by Amerindian people, Taino, Siboney, Carib, Arawak.

In 1492, Columbus "discovered" (as it is said) the Caribbean, and with that discovery came the intrusion of European culture and peoples and a fragmentation of the original Amerindian culture. We had Europe "nationalizing" itself, and there were Spanish, French, English, and Dutch conquerors so that people had to start speaking (and thinking in) four metropolitan languages rather than possibly a single native language. Then with the destruction of the Amerindians, which took place within thirty years of Columbus's discovery (one million dead a year), it was necessary for the Europeans to import new labor bodies into the Caribbean. And the most convenient form of labor was the labor on the very edge of the trade winds—the labor on the edge of the slave trade winds, the labor on the edge of the hurricane, the labor on the edge of West Africa. And so the peoples of Ashanti, Congo, Nigeria, from all that mighty coast of western Africa were imported into the Caribbean. And we had the arrival in that area of a new language structure. It consisted of many languages, but basically they had a common

*This talk was presented at Harvard late in August 1979. Hurricanes ravish the Caribbean and the southern coasts of the United States in the summer of every year.

semantic and stylistic form.[2] What these languages had to do, however, was to submerge themselves, because officially the conquering peoples—the Spaniards, the English, the French, and the Dutch—insisted that the language of public discourse and conversation, of obedience, command, and reception, should be English, French, Spanish, or Dutch. They did not wish to hear people speaking Ashanti or any of the Congolese languages. So there was a submergence of this imported language. Its status became one of inferiority. Similarly, its speakers were slaves. They were conceived of as inferiors—nonhuman, in fact. But this very submergence served an interesting intercultural purpose, because although people continued to speak English as it was spoken in Elizabethan times and on through the Romantic and Victorian ages, that English was, nonetheless, still being influenced by the underground language, the submerged language that the slaves had brought. And that underground language was itself constantly transforming itself into new forms. It was moving from a purely African form to a form that was African, but which was adapted to the new environment and adapted to the cultural imperative of the European languages. And it was influencing the way in which the French, Dutch, and Spanish spoke their own languages. So there was a very complex process taking place, which is now beginning to surface in our literature.

In the Caribbean, as in South Africa (and in any area of cultural imperialism for that matter), the educational system did not recognize the presence of these various languages. What our educational system did was to recognize and maintain the language of the conquistador—the language of the planter, the language of the official, the language of the Anglican preacher. It insisted that not only would English be spoken in the Anglophone Caribbean, but that the educational system would carry the contours of an English heritage. Hence, as Dennis said, Shakespeare, George Eliot, Jane Austen—British literature and literary forms, the models that were intimate to Europe, that were intimate to Great Britain, that had very little to do, really, with the environment and the reality of the Caribbean—were dominant in the Caribbean educational system. It was a very surprising situation. People were forced to learn things that had no relevance to themselves. Paradoxically, in the Caribbean (as in many other "cultural disaster" areas), the people educated in this system came to know more, even today, about English kings and queens than they do about our own national heroes, our own slave rebels—the people who helped to build and to destroy our society. We are more excited by English literary models, by the concept of, say, Sherwood Forest and Robin Hood, than we are by Nanny of the Maroons, a name some of us didn't even know until a few years ago.[3] And in terms of what we write, our perceptual models, we are more conscious (in terms of sensibility) of the falling of snow for instance—the models are all there for the falling of the snow—than of the force of the hurricanes that take place every year. In other words, we haven't got the syllables, the syllabic intelligence, to describe the hurricane, which is our own experience;[4] whereas we can describe the imported alien experience of the snowfall. It is that kind of situation that we are in.

Now the Creole adaptation to that is the little child who, instead of writing in an essay "The snow was falling on the fields of Shropshire" (which is what our children literally were writing until a few years ago, below drawings they made of white snow fields and the corn-haired people who inhabited such a landscape), wrote "The snow was falling on the cane fields."[5] The child had not yet reached the obvious statement that it wasn't snow at all, but rain that was probably falling on the cane fields. She was trying to have both cultures at the same time. But that is creolization.

What is even more important, as we develop this business of emergent language in the Caribbean, is the actual rhythm and the syllables, the very body work, in a way, of the language. What English has given us as a model for poetry, and to a lesser extent, prose (but poetry is the basic tool here), is the pentam-

eter: "The cúrfew tólls the knéll of párting dáy." There have,
of course, been attempts to break it. And there were other
dominant forms like, for example, *Beowulf* (c. 750), *The Sea-
farer,* and what Langland (1322?–1400?) had produced:

> For trewthe telleth that love. is triacle of hevene;
> May no synne be on him sene. that useth that spise,
> And alle his werkes he wrougte. with love as him liste.

Or, from *Piers the Plowman* (which does not make it into
Palgrave's Golden Treasury, but which we all had to "do" at
school) the haunting prologue:

> In a somer seson. whan soft was the sonne
> I shope me into shroudes. as I a shepe were

which has recently inspired our own Derek Walcott with his
first major nation language effort:

> In idle August, while the sea soft,
> and leaves of brown islands stick to the rim
> of this Caribbean, I blow out the light
> by the dreamless face of Maria Concepcion
> to ship as a seaman on the schooner *Flight*.[6]

But by the time we reach Chaucer (1345–1400), the pentameter
prevails. Over in the New World, the Americans—Walt Whitman—
tried to bridge or to break the pentameter through a cosmic
movement, a large movement of sound. Cummings tried to fragment it. And Marianne Moore attacked it with syllabics. But
basically the pentameter remained, and it carries with it a certain kind of experience, which is not the experience of a hurricane. The hurricane does not roar in pentameter. And that's
the problem: how do you get a rhythm that approximates the
natural experience, the environmental experience? We have
been trying to break out of the entire pentametric model in the
Caribbean and to move into a system that more closely and intimately approaches our own experience. So that is what we
are talking about now.

It is nation language in the Caribbean that, in fact, largely ignores the pentameter. Nation language is the language that is influenced very strongly by the African model, the African aspect of our New World/Caribbean heritage. English it may be in terms of its lexicon, but it is not English in terms of its syntax. And English it certainly is not in terms of its rhythm and timbre, its own sound explosion. In its contours, it is not English, even though the words, as you hear them, would be English to a greater or lesser degree. And this brings us back to the question that some of you raised yesterday: can English be a revolutionary language? And the lovely answer that came back was: it is not English that is the agent. It is not language, but people, who make revolutions.

I think, however, that language does really have a role to play here, certainly in the Caribbean. But it is an English that is not the standard, imported, educated English, but that of the submerged, surrealist experience and sensibility, which has always been there and which is now increasingly coming to the surface and influencing the perception of contemporary Caribbean people. It is what I call, as I say, *nation language.* I use the term in contrast to *dialect.* The word dialect has been bandied about for a long time, and it carries very pejorative overtones. Dialect is thought of as bad English. Dialect is "inferior English." Dialect is the language when you want to make fun of someone. Caricature speaks in dialect. Dialect has a long history coming from the plantation where people's dignity is distorted through their language and the descriptions that the dialect gave to them. Nation language, on the other hand, is the submerged area of that dialect that is much more closely allied to the African aspect of experience in the Caribbean. It may be in English, but often it is in an English which is like a howl, or a shout, or a machine-gun, or the wind, or a wave. It is also like the blues. And sometimes it is English and African at the same time. I am going to give you some examples. But I should tell you that the reason I have to talk so much is that there has been very little

written about our nation language. I bring you to the notion of
nation language but I can refer you to very little literature, to
very few resources. I cannot refer you to what you call an *establishment*. I cannot really refer you to authorities because
there aren't any.[7] One of our urgent tasks now is to try to create our own authorities. But I will give you a few ideas of what
people have tried to do.

The forerunner of all this was, of course, Dante Alighieri
who, at the beginning of the fourteenth century, argued, in *De
vulgari eloquentia* (1304), for the recognition of the (his own)
Tuscan vernacular as the nation language to replace Latin as
the most natural, complete, and accessible means of verbal expression. And the movement was, in fact, successful throughout
Europe with the establishment of national languages and litera-
tures. But these very successful national languages then pro-
ceeded to ignore local European colonial languages such as
Basque and Gaelic, and to suppress overseas colonial languages
wherever they were heard. And it was not until the appearance
of Burns in the eighteenth century and Rothenberg, Trask,
Vansina, Tedlock, Waley, Walton, Whallon, Jahn, Jones, White-
ly, Beckwith, Herskovitz, and Ruth Finnegan, among many
others in this century, that we have returned, at least to the
notion of oral literature, although I don't need to remind you
that oral literature is our oldest form of "auriture" and that it
continues richly throughout the world today.[8]

In the Caribbean, our novelists have always been conscious of
these native resources, but the critics and academics have, as is
often the case, lagged far behind. Indeed, until 1970, there was
a positive intellectual, almost social, hostility to the concept of
dialect as language. But there were some significant studies in
linguistics, such as Beryl Lofton Bailey's *Jamaican Creole Syntax: A Transformational Approach*; also: F. G. Cassidy, *Jamaica
Talk*; Cassidy and R. B. LePage, *Dictionary of Jamaican English*;
and, still to come, Richard Allsopp's mind-blowing *Dictionary
of Caribbean English*. There are three glossaries from Frank
Collymore in Barbados and A. J. Seymour and John R. Rick-

ford of Guyana; and studies on the African presence in Caribbean language by Mervyn Alleyne, Beverley Hall, and Maureen Warner Lewis.[9] In addition, there has been work by Douglas Taylor and Cicely John, among others, on aspects of some of the Amerindian languages; and Dennis Craig, Laurence Carrington, Velma Pollard, and several others at the University of the West Indies's School of Education have done some work on the structure of nation language and its psychosomosis in and for the classroom.

Few of the writers mentioned, however, have gone into nation language as it affects literature. They have set out its grammar, syntax, transformation, structure, and all of those things. But they haven't really been able to make any contact between the nation language and its expression in our literature. Recently, a French poet and novelist from Martinique, Edouard Glissant, had a remarkable article in *Alcheringa,* a nation language journal published at Boston University. The article was called "Free and Forced Poetics," and in it, for the first time, I feel an effort to describe what nation language really means.[10] For the author of the article it is the language of enslaved persons. For him, nation language is a strategy: the slave is forced to use a certain kind of language in order to disguise himself, to disguise his personality, and to retain his culture. And he defines that language as "forced poetics" because it is a kind of prison language, if you want to call it that.

And then we have another nation language poet, Bruce St. John, from Barbados, who has written some informal introductions to his own work which describe the nature of the experiments that he is conducting and the kind of rules that he begins to perceive in the way that he uses his language.[11]

I myself have an article called "Jazz and the West Indian novel," which appeared in a journal called *Bim* in the early 1960s,[12] and there I attempt to show that the connection between native musical structures and the native language is very necessary to the understanding of nation language. That music is, in fact, the surest threshold to the language that comes out of it.[13]

So that is all we have to offer as authority, which isn't very much, really. But that is how it is. And in fact, one characteristic of nation language is its orality. It is from "the oral tradition." And therefore you wouldn't really expect that large, encyclopedic body of learned comment on it that you would expect for a written language and literature.

Now I'd like to describe for you some of the characteristics of our nation language. First of all it is from, as I've said, an oral tradition. The poetry, the culture itself, exists not in a dictionary but in the tradition of the spoken word. It is based as much on sound as it is on song. That is to say, the noise that it makes is part of the meaning, and if you ignore the noise (or what you would think of as noise, shall I say), then you lose part of the meaning. When it is written, you lose the sound or the noise, and therefore you lose part of the meaning. Which is, again, why I have to have a tape recorder for this presentation. I want you to get the sound of it, rather than the sight of it.

Now in order to break down the pentameter, we discovered an ancient form which was always there, the calypso.[14] This is a form that I think everyone knows about. It does not employ the iambic pentameter. It employs dactyls. It therefore mandates the use of the tongue in a certain way, the use of sound in a certain way. It is a model that we are moving naturally toward now.

(Iambic Pentameter)	To be or not to be, that is the question
(Kaiso)	The stone had skidded arc'd and bloomed into islands
	Cuba San Domingo
	Jamaica Puerto Rico

But not only is there a difference in syllabic or stress pattern, there is an important difference in shape of intonation. In the Shakespeare (above), the voice travels in a single forward plane toward the horizon of its end. In the kaiso, after the skimming movement of the first line, we have a distinct variation. The voice dips and deepens to describe an intervallic pattern. And then there are more ritual forms like *kumina*, like *shango*, the religious forms,[15] which I won't have time to go into here, but which begin to disclose the complexity that is possible with nation language. What I am attempting to do this morning is to give you a kind of vocabulary introduction to nation language, rather than an analysis of its more complex forms. But I want to make the point that the forms are capable of remarkable complexity, and if there were time I could take you through some of the more complex musical/literary forms as well.

The other thing about nation language is that it is part of what may be called *total expression,* a notion that is not unfamiliar to you because you are coming back to that kind of thing now. Reading is an isolated, individualistic expression. The oral tradition, on the other hand, makes demands not only on the poet but also on the audience to complete the community: the noise and sounds that the poet makes are responded to by the audience and are returned to him. Hence we have the creation of a continuum where the meaning truly resides. And this total expression comes about because people live in the open air, because people live in conditions of poverty, because people come from a historical experience where they had to rely on their own breath patterns rather than on paraphernalia like books and museums. They had to depend on *immanence,* the power within themselves, rather than the technology outside themselves.

Let me begin by playing for you, first of all, some West Indian poets who are writing in standard English, or if you like, in West Indian standard English. The first poet is Claude McKay, who some people think of as American. He appears in American anthologies, especially anthologies of black writing. (Until recently, American anthologies hardly ever contained black writers, except perhaps Phillis Wheatley.) But McKay (1889–

1940) was born in Jamaica and was a policeman in the constabulary there for some years before emigrating to the States where he quickly became a leading figure in what has come to be known as the Harlem Renaissance. But although he is very much identified with the black movement, he was, except perhaps during the most productive years of his life, rather ambivalent about his negritude.[16] And in this recording made toward the end of his life in the forties, when he had moved from communism to catholicism, for instance, he is saying, in this lead-in to his most famous and militant poem, "If we must die," a banner poem if ever there was one (it is a counter-lynching poem), that he is a *poet,* not a *black* poet, and not, as he said in those days, a "coloured" poet. And he goes on to recount the story of how a copy of "If we must die" was found on the body of a dead (white) soldier during the First World War. The newspapers recorded the occasion and everyone started quoting the poem. But no one, McKay says, said—"perhaps they did not even know"—that he was black. Which was okay by him, he says, because it helped ensure his "universality." (Winston Churchill also quoted this poem—without attributing it to the author who, when he had gone to Bernard Shaw for encouragement in earlier days, had been advised by the Grand Old Man [after Shaw had taken a shrewd look at him] that he'd better try it as a boxer!)

Well, that's the first stage and story of our literature. We want to be universal, to be universally accepted. But it's the terrible terms meted out for universality that interest me. In order to be "universal" McKay forsook his nation language, forshook his early mode of poetry and went to the sonnet.[17] And his sonnet, "St Isaac's Church, Petrograd," is a poem that could have been written by a European, perhaps most intimately by a Russian in Petrograd. It certainly could have been written by any poet of the post-Victorian era. The only thing that retains its uniqueness here (in terms of my notion of nation language) is the tone of the poet's voice. But the form and the content are very closely connected to European models. This does not mean that it is a bad poem or that I am putting it down. I am merely saying that, aesthetically, there are no unique elements in this poem apart from the voice of the poet reciting his own poem. And I will have a musical model that will appear after you have listened to the poem, and you can tell me whether you think I am fair or not. (On tape: McKay reading his sonnet followed by the "Agnus Dei" from Fauré's *Requiem*.)

> Bow down my soul in worship very low
> And in the holy silences be lost
> Bow down before the marble Man of Woe,
> Bow down before the singing angel host . . .[18]

The only trouble is that McKay had "trouble" with his syllables, his Clarendon syllables are very "evident," and he didn't always say "the," but sometimes said "de," which is a form in nation language. And these elisions, the sound of them, subtly erode, somewhat, the classical pentametric of the sonnet. . . .

Our second poet is George Campbell, also of Jamaica. In 1945, Jamaica was, after a long history of struggle, granted by Britain the right to move toward self-government and independence with a new political constitution and the formation of the People's National Party. George Campbell was very moved by, and involved in, these events, and he wrote what I consider his finest poem:

> On this momentous night O God help us.
> With faith we now challenge our destiny.
> Tonight masses of men will shape, will hope,
> Will dream with us; so many years hang on
> Acceptance. Why is that knocking against
> The door?.......is it you
> Looking for a destiny, or is it
> Noise of the storm?[19]

Now you see here a man who is becoming conscious of his

nationality. But when he comes to write his greatest poem, he is still writing a Miltonic ode; or perhaps it is because he's writing his greatest poem, that it must be given that kind of nobility.[20] And it is read by our Milton of the Caribbean, George Lamming, our great organ voice, a voice that Lamming himself, in his book *The Pleasures of Exile* (1960) recognizes as one of the finest in English orature. But the point is that from my perspective, George Campbell's ode, fittingly read by George Lamming, isn't giving us any unique element in terms of the Caribbean environment. But it is still a beautiful poem wonderfully read. (On tape: Lamming reading Campbell's poem. . . .)

> Must the horse rule the rider or the man
> The horse.
> Wind where cometh the fine technique
> Of rule passing through me? My hands wet with
> The soil and I knowing my world

> [The reading was followed by the opening of Beethoven's Fifth Symphony] [21]

The models are important here, you see. The McKay can be matched with Fauré, Campbell/Lamming with Beethoven. What follows next on the tape, however, is equally important because our local Beethoven employs a completely different model. I'm not saying his model is equal to the Fifth Symphony, but it makes a similar statement, and it gets us into what I now consider the nation or native language. Big Yout's sound poem, "Salaman Agundy," begins with a scream (On tape: Big Yout's "Screamin' Target"/"Salaman Agundy" from the LP *Screamin' Target* [Kingston, c. 1972]), followed by the bass-based reggae canter of downbeat on the first "syllable" of the first and second bars, followed by a syncopation on the third third, followed by full offbeat/downbeats in the fourth:

The other model that we have, and that we have always had in the Caribbean, is the calypso, and we are going to hear now the Mighty Sparrow singing a kaiso which came out in the early sixties. It marked, in fact, the first major change in consciousness that we all shared. And Sparrow made a criticism of all that I and Dennis have been saying about the educational system. In "Dan is the Man in the Van" he says that the education we get from England has really made us idiots because all of those things that we had to read about: Robin Hood, King Alfred and the Cakes, King Arthur and the Knights of the Round Table, all of these things really haven't given us anything but empty words. And he did it in the calypso form. And you should hear the rhyme scheme of this poem. He is rhyming on "n's" and "l's," and he is creating a cluster of syllables and a counterpoint between voice and orchestra, between individual and community, within the formal notion of "call and response," which becomes typical of our nation in the revolution.

(Solo) Acordin to de education you get   when you small
        You(ll) grow up wi(th) true ambition an respec for one an all
        But in MY days in school   they teach me like a fool
        THE THINGS THEY TEACH ME A SHOULDA BEEN A
        BLOCK-HEADED MULE

(Chorus) *Pussy has finish his work long ago*
          An now he restin an ting
          Solomon Agundy was born on a MunDEE
          DE ASS IN DE LION SKIN....[22]

I could bring you a book, *The Royal Reader,* or the one referred to by Sparrow, *Nelson's West Indian Reader* by J. O. Cutteridge, that we had to learn at school by heart. It contained phrases like: "the cow jumped over the moon," "ding dong bell, pussy in the well," and so on. I mean, that was our beginning of an understanding of literature. Literature started (startled, really) literally at that level, with that kind of model. The problem of transcending this is what I am talking about now.

A more complex form by Sparrow is this next poem, "Ten to

One Is Murder." Now it's interesting how this goes, because
Sparrow has been accused of shooting someone on the eve of
Carnival, just before Lent. (Kaiso and Carnival are two of our
great folk expressions.) Now Sparrow apparently shot someone, but because of the popular nature of the calypsonian, he
was able to defend himself long before he got into court by
creating the scenario for the reason why he shot the man. He
shot the man, he says, because for no reason at all, ten irates
suddenly appear one night, surround him, and started throwing
stones. The one in front was a very good pelter, and Sparrow
didn't know what to do. He couldn't even find shelter. So he
ran and ran and ran until finally he remembered that he had a
gun (a wedger) in his pocket. He was forced to take it out and
shoot *pow pow pow* and the crowd start to scatter. As a result
he had the community on his side before the trial even started.
But even if he hadn't written the song, he would have had the
community on his side because here you have a folk poet; and
folk poets are the spokesmen whose whole concern is to express
the experiences of the people rather than the experiences of the
elite. But here is "Ten to One Is Murder." Each slash phrase is
an impressionistic brush stroke:

> About ten in de night on de fifth of October
> *Ten to One is Murder!*
> Way down Henry Street, up by H. G. M. Walker
> *Ten to One is Murder!*
> Well, de leader of de gang was a lot like a pepperrr
> *Ten to One is Murder!*
> An every man in de gang had a white-handle razorrr
> *Ten to One is Murder!*
> They say ah push a gal from Grenada
> *Ten to One is Murder! . . .*[23]

Now that is dramatic monologue which, because of its call-
and-response structure (in addition, of course, to its own in-
trinsic drama), is capable of extension on stage. There is in fact
a tent form known as calypso drama, which calls upon Trini-

dadian nation forms like *grand charge, picong, robber talk,* and so on, which Sparrow is in fact consciously using in this calypso, and which some of the younger Trinidadian nation poets like Malik, Questel, and Christopher Laird, for example, are bringing into play in their poetry.

Man a start to sweat. Man a soakin wet
Mama so much threat: that's a night a can never forget
Ten to One is Murder! . . .

Next we have the poet who has been writing nation all her life and who, because of that, has been ignored until recently: the poet Louise Bennett (Miss Lou) of Jamaica. Now this is very interesting because she is middle class, and "middle class" means brown, urban, respectable, and standard English, and "the snow was falling in the canefields."[24] It certainly doesn't mean an entrenched economic/political position, as in Europe. For instance, Miss Lou's mother's and Miss Lou's own upbringing was "rural St Mary," hence the honorable Louise's natural and rightful knowledge of the folk.[25] (It was not until the post-independence seventies that she was officially—as distinct from popularly—recognized and given the highest honors, including the right to the title of Honorable.) But one is supposed, as V. S. Naipaul once said at a memorable Writers Conference in Jamaica, to graduate out of these things;[26] therefore there is no reason why Louise should have persisted with Anancy and Auntie Roachie and *boonoonoonoos* an *parangles* an *ting,* when she could have opted for "And how are you today," the teeth and lips tight and closed around the mailed fist of a smile. But her instincts were that she should use the language of her people. The consequence was that for years (since 1936?) she performed her work in crowded village halls across the island, and until 1945 could get nothing accepted by the *Gleaner,* the island's largest, oldest (estab. 1854), and often only newspaper. (Claude McKay had been published in Kingston, including in the *Gleaner,* in 1912, but he had had an influential white sponsor, the Englishman Walter Jeckyll, compiler of *Jamaican Song and Story* [1907].)[27] And although by 1962 she had already published nine books,[28] Miss Lou does not appear among the poets in the *Independent Anthology of Jamaican Poetry,* but is at the back of the book, like an afterthought if not an embarrassment, under "Miscellaneous." She could not be accepted, even at the moment of political independence, as a poet. Though all this, as I say, is dramatically altered now with the Revolution of the late sixties, her consciousness of this unfortunate situation remains where it hurts most: "I have been set apart by other creative writers a long time ago because of the language I speak and work in . . . From the beginning nobody recognized me as a writer."[29] I couldn't satisfactorily reproduce in print Miss Lou's "Street Cries" played for the lecture from her long-playing album *Miss Lou's Views.*[30] Here instead are two examples of her more "formal" verse from the book collection *Jamaica Labrish,* recordings from which, Miss Lou informs me, should be available alongside the revised edition of *Labrish* quite soon.[31] First, "Pedestrian Crosses":

If a cross yuh dah-cross,
Beg yuh cross mek me pass.
Dem yah crossin' is crosses yuh know!
Koo de line! Yuh noh se
Cyar an truck backa me?
Hear dah hoganeer one deh dah-blow!

Missis, walk fas' an cross!
Pickney, cross mek me pass!
Lady, galang an mine yuh business!
Ole man mek up yuh mine
Walk between dem white line!
Wat a crosses dem crossin yah is!

. . .

De crossin a-stop we from pass mek dem cross,
But nutten dah-stop dem from cross mek we pass,
Dem yah crossin is crosses fe true![32]

And "Dutty Tough" begins:

> Sun a-shine but tings noh bright,
> Doah pot a-bwile, bickle noh nuff,
> River flood but water scarce yaw,
> Rain a-fall but dutty tuff!

And ends on this note of social commentary:

> De price o' bread gan up so high
> Dat we haffe agree,
> Fe cut we y'eye pon bread an all
> Tun dumplin refugee!

> An all dem mawga smaddy weh
> Dah-gwan like fat is sin,
> All dem deh weh dah-fas' wid me,
> Ah lef dem to dumplin!

> Sun a-shine an pot a-bwile, but
> Ting noh bright, bickle noh nuff!
> Rain a-fall, river dah-flood, but
> Wata scarce an dutty tuff![33]

These are the models that we have, and I could give you more complex examples than the ones you have so far heard. What I am going to do now, however, since there is a constraint on time for this session, is give you an idea of how the "mainstream" anglophone Caribbean poets reached the stage signalled by Miss Lou.

The mainstream poets who were moving from standard English to nation language were influenced basically, I think (again the models are important), by T. S. Eliot. What T. S. Eliot did for Caribbean poetry and Caribbean literature was to introduce the notion of the speaking voice, the conversational tone.[34] That is what really attracted us to Eliot. And you can see how the Caribbean poets introduced here have been influenced by him, although they eventually went on to create their own environmental expression.

The first poet (writing in the forties) is a magistrate and historian from Barbados, called H. A. Vaughan, and he is reading a sonnet called "For Certain Demogogues." It is a "standard English" poem except for a passage toward the end when the image of blackbirds appears. Here, suddenly for the first time, and rare in Vaughan's poetry, he imitates the sound and the motion, the movement of the hopping of these peculiar birds and gets this into his poetry, which becomes one of the first and early stages of nation language: *mimesis*. In fact, had I not heard this poem, I might never have "recognized" it.

> 'We *love* the people, sir!' You do?
>   You ought to! nay, indeed, you must
> Shouting their needs has brought a new
>   Elation to your fickle dust
>
> . . . .
>
> You prey, but not like *beasts* of prey;
>   The cobblers fly too far to be
> Your emblem; in a higgling way
>   You have a place in history;
>
> *Like blackbirds in their shiny coats*
>   *Prinking and lifting spry, proud feet,*
> *Bickering and picking sodden oats*
>   *From horses' offal in the street.*[35]

Now we must also hear from Frank Collymore,[36] who is a schoolmaster and editor of the magazine *Bim* that I mentioned earlier. Here is the conversational tone of the early fifties. He is talking about going back to school and the materialist dangers of scholastic education, continuing the theme, in fact, that is being raised by Dennis Brutus's lecture, and Sparrow's calypso, and Big Yout's "Salaman Agundy," but getting it all into a wonderfully achieved conversational style and tone. There is, however, no nation language as such here; no unique element similar to Vaughan's "blackbirds," for instance. But the conversational mode can have a corrosive effect on the tyranny of the pentameter:

In a couple of weeks' time school will reopen
    If not with a flourish of trumpets at least with a shout
From the several hundred boys gathered together in the building,
    And though a few perhaps may wonder what it's all about . . .
The fuss of education, I mean . . . their parents and the others
    Who have to fit the bill of books and shoes
Will be prouder than ever that their young are well on the road
    To knowledge—not that they'll be caring particularly who's
Going to dish out the stuff, or even what it is for that matter,
    Only the platters have got to be picked clean,
And afterwards with the School Certificate nicely framed
    And the New Order hovering suspiciously near the scene!
French irregular verbs, quadratic equations,
    Maybe a century in the First Division . . . who knows?
And for those who can't take it all in by the prescribed method
    There's a road to the brain through the backside by blows. . . .[37]

Our third established poet, John Figueroa, writing in the late sixties, now begins to use nation language, and he uses it as a very self-conscious and formal contrast to standard English, as a reaction, no doubt, to the folk/nation rupture (I won't say irruption, though some hoped that it was merely an *interruption*) that had taken place in our poetry with the publication of my *Rights of Passage* (London, 1967), and the effects of the great literary debate that had taken place a few years before that on the issue of literature and dialect (1965) when it was demonstrated, for perhaps the first time (at last), that a nation language poem could be serious and employ not only semantic but sound elements: in this case, the sound-structure of Rastafarian drums and the "Dry Bones" spiritual:

Watch *dem* ship *dem*
come to *town* dem

full o' *silk* dem
full o' *food* dem

an' *dem* plane *dem*
come to *groun'* dem

full o' *flash* dem
full o' *cash* dem

silk *dem* food *dem*
shoe *dem* wine *dem*

dat *dem* drink *dem*
an consume *dem*

praisin' de glory of the Lord. . . .[38]

This "riddmic" aspect of Caribbean nation language was to
be further extended in the late seventies by the Jamaican
reggae/dub poets Oku Onoura (Orlando Wong), Michael Smith
(whom we shall hear from later), and Linton Kwesi Johnson of
Black London. This is from "Five Nights of Bleedin" from
Johnson's LP *Dread Beat an Blood*:

night number one was in BRIX/TON:
SOFRANO B sounn sys/tem
was a-beatin out a riddim/ wid a fy*ah*,
commin doun his reggae-reggae wy*ah*;

it was a sounn shakin doun you spinal col/umn,
a bad music tearin up you *flesh*;
an th'rebels-dem start a-fightin,
th'yout dem jus tunn *wild*.

it's war amongst th'rebels:
mad/ness . . . mad/ness . . . *war.* . . .

and

so wid a flick
a de wrist
a jab an a stab

th'song of blades was *soun*/ded
th'bile of oppression was *vom*/ited
an *two* policemen *woun*/ded

righteous righteous war.[39]

But nation language isn't confined, as you must have recognized by now, to rhythmic variations. Miss Lou follows the tra-

ditional Scots tune very nicely, thank you, with her "Every
secky got him jeggeh/Every puppy got him flea"; while I got
pretty close to Bajan country speech (free cadence and vocabulary) in "The Dust," also from *Rights of Passage,* where
some women are recalling a volcanic irruption in another island:

> Some say
> is in one o' dem islands away
>
> where they language tie-tongue
> an' to hear them speak so
> in they St Lucia patois
> is as if they cahn unnerstan'
>
> a single word o' English.
> But uh doan really know. All uh know
> is that one day suddenly so
> this mountain leggo one *brugg-a-lung-go*
>
> whole bloody back side
> o' this hill like it blow
> off like they blastin' stones
> in de quarry.
>
> Rocks big as you cow pen hois'
> in de air as if they was one
> set o' shingles. That noise,
> Jesus Chrise, mussa rain down
>
> splinter an' spark
> as if it was Con-
> federation.[40]

The roots and underground link to all these emerging forces
was the now almost legendary Rastafarian poet, Bongo Jerry,
whose revolutionary mis/use of Babylonian English was practically apocalyptic:

MABRAK

> Lightning
> is the future brightening,
> for last year man learn

how to use black eyes.
(wise!)

MABRAK:
                    NEWSFLASH!
"Babylon plans crash"
Thunder interrupt their programme to
announce:

BLACK ELECTRIC STORM
                                        IS HERE

How long you feel "fair to fine"
(WHITE) would last?

How long in darkness
          when out of BLACK
          come forth LIGHT?

MABRAK is righting the wrongs and brain-whitening . . .
Not just by washing out the straightening and wearing dashiki t'ing:

MOSTOFTHESTRAIGHTENINGISINTHETONGUE—so . . .

Save the YOUNG
from the language that MEN teach,
the doctrine Pope preach
skin bleach. . . .

                    MAN must use MEN language
                    to carry dis message:

SILENCE BABEL TONGUES; recall and
recollect BLACK SPEECH.[41]

Now Figueroa's nation language, and that of many of the
other established poets who followed, was very likely a reaction
to (and against) all this. But it all had its effect, its influence;
though the difference at this stage between Figueroa/main-
stream and the natives (the cultural gorillas) per se, was that,
while for the natives nation language informs the very shape
and spirit of their poems, for Figueroa in "Portrait of a Woman,"
for instance, the control and narrative, the "classical," even
Prosperian element—the most part of the poem—is in English.
The marginal bit, that of the voice and status of the domestic

helper, the house slave, Caliban's sister, is in nation, but a nation still sticky and wet with dialect; though Figueroa might claim that the glory of Caribbean English is that it has a wide range of resources and we should use them all:

> Firmly, sweetly
> refusing . . .
>
> Tall for seventeen fit
> for a tumble
>
>> (*'A guess hard time*
>> *tek er'*) she said
>> referring to
>> her mother's misfortune
>> (Her strict mother whose
>> three men had left
>> her holding five pledges to fortune.)
>
> She came easily into
> my arms
> refusing only to kiss
>> (*'any familiarity an*
>> *we stop right now'*)
>
> Dixerat—as lacrymae rerum used to say.
> She's in the public domain
> she's lost her patent rights . . .
>
>> '*You have bad min'*
>> *doan tell nobody*
>> *doan tell nobody*
>> *doan mek me do it*
>>> *mek mi*
>> *doan mek me do it*
>>> *mek mi*
>>> *lawd!*
>> You see I intend to be
>>> a nurse'
>> No need to apologise
>> (*Lawd it sweet !*)
>> 'But if you try to kiss
>> me I will scream.'[42]

Next Derek Walcott, the Caribbean's most accomplished
poet/playwright, with a poem about a little night-violence in
New York called "Blues," which is not a blues at all; it doesn't
have that form. But it is a wonderfully speech-textured piece,
giving form to Collymore's conversational style. And the blues
is there in Walcott's voice. You will hear in his reading the
sound of Don Drummond's trombone. . . .

> Those five or six young guys
> hunched on the stoop
> that oven-hot summer night
> whistled me over. Nice
> and friendly. So I stop.
> MacDougal or Christopher
> Street in chains of light. . . .[43]

Don Drummond, Jamaican ghetto/culture hero of the fifties
and early sixties, was a jazz musician of genius (I would com-
pare him with J. J. Johnson) who was, at the same time, one of
the originators of *ska,* the native sound at the yardway of the
cultural revolution that would lead eventually to Bob Marley,
reggae, and *The Harder They Come.*[44] It is a connection of
Caribbean and Harlem/New Orleans which Buddy Bolden and
Congo Square knew about, which McKay was to carry forward,
and which in this poem, among some others (see especially *The
Gulf*), Derek Walcott continues. And it is this connection which
brings in the influences of Langston Hughes for instance, and
Imamu Baraka, and Sonia Sanchez, and Miles Davis, which further erodes the pentameter. . . .

> My face smashed in, my bloody mug
> pouring, my olive-branch jacket saved
> from cuts and tears,
> I crawled four flights upstairs. . . .
>
>   I
> remember a few watchers waved
> loudly, and one kid's mother shouting
> like 'Jackie' or 'Terry',

'Now that's enough!'
It's nothing really.
They don't get enough love.

You know they wouldn't kill
you. Just playing rough
like young America will.
Still, it taught me something
about love. If it's so tough,
forget it.[45]

Today we have a very confident movement of nation language. In fact, it is inconceivable that any Caribbean poet
writing today is not going to be influenced by this submerged
culture, which is, in fact, an emerging culture. And it is obvious now to most Caribbean writers, I would say, except perhaps some of the exiled,[46] that one has to communicate with
the audience. No one is going to assert that a poet cannot live
in his ivory tower, or that a poet cannot be an individual—all
that we have been through already. But the point is that for
the needs of the kind of emerging society that I am defending—
for the people who have had to recite "The boy /stood on /the
burn /ing deck" for so long, who are unable to express the
power of the hurricane in the way that they write their words—
at last our poets today are recognizing that it is essential that
they use the resources that have always been there, but which
have been denied to them—which they have sometimes themselves denied.

I shall end with the violet and red extremes of the spectrum.
Here, first, is fundamental nation, the language of a *kumina*
queen, with its *kikongo* base. Again, although there is no question about the beauty and power of Miss Queenie's language
and images—she is, after all, priestess, prophet, and symbolist,
without hearing her (seeing her of course completes the experience because then you would know how she uses her eyes, her
mouth, her whole face; how her arms encircle or reject; how her

fingers can become water or spear), but without hearing her,
you would miss the dynamics of the narrative—the blue notes
of that voice; its whispers and pauses and repetitions and stut-
ters and eleisons; its high pitch emphases and its low pitched
trails; and that hoarse quality which I suppose you know from
Nina Simone. With Miss Queenie we are in the very ancient
dawn of nation language, and to be able to come to terms with
oral literature at all our critics must be able to understand the
complex forces that have led to this classical expression. . . .

> One day...
> a remember one day a faen some lillies...
> an a plant de lillies-dem in row
> an one Sunday mornin when a wake...
> all de lillies blow...
> *seven* lillies an de seven a dem blow...
>
> an a *leave*...
> an guh dung in de gully bottom...
> to go an pick some quoquonut
> an when a go
> a see a cottn tree an a juss *fell* right down...
> at de cottn tree root...
>
> . . . .
>
> in de night
> in de cottn tree comin like it holloow
> an Hi hinside there
> an you have some grave arounn dat cottn tree
> right rounn it
> some *tombs*...
>
> but dose is
> some hol-time Hafrican
> yu unnerstann . . .?
>
> well dose tombs arounn de cottn tree...
> an Hi inside de cottn tree lay down
> an a night-time a sih de cotton tree *light* hup wit cyandles an...
> a restin now
> put me an *dis* way an sleepin...

an a honly hear a likkle *vice*
come to mih
an dem talkin to mih
but dose tings is spirit talkin to mih...
an dem speakin to me now
an seh now...

'Is a likkle *nice* likkle chile
an oo gwine get im right up now...
in de Hafrican worl...
because you brains
you will *take* someting...
so derefore...
we gine to *teach* you someting...'

Well de *firs* ting dat dem teach me is
s'*wikkidi*...

s'*wikkidi lango*
which is sugar an water...

sih?
an dem teach me dat...

an dem teach me m'praey-ers...
which is...

> *Kwale kwale n'den den de*
> *Bele ko lo mawa kisalaya*
>
> *Pem legele*
> *Len legele*
>
> *Luwi za'kwe n'da'kwe so*
> *Be'lam m'pese m'bambe*

which is de same Hour Fader's Praeyer. . . .[47]

Michael Smith (b. Kingston, Jamaica, 1954) is such an intransigent sound poet that he's not concerned with written
script at all. He "publishes," like a calypsonian, at his public
poetry readings at Zinc Fence Theatre or School of Drama audi-
torium or, like the early Louise Bennett, in all the large or little
places throughout Jamaica where he's constantly invited to appear. But whereas it was years before Louise was recognized,

Smith, like Bob Marley and the reggae kings (almost a tautology), is a pop star, as are Oku Onoura and Paul Keens-Douglas, two other very popular sound poets who have actually appeared in performance with Marley and Tosh and Sparrow. The sound/poems of Linton Kwesi Johnson are on the charts in Great Britain.[48] For these inheritors of the revolution, nation language is no longer anything to argue about or experiment with; it is their classical norm and comes out of the same experience as the music of contemporary popular song. They use the same "riddims," the same voice spreads, syllable clusters, blue notes, ostinato, syncopation, and pauses, along with, in Smith's case, a quite remarkable voice and breath control, accompanied by a decorative S90 *noise* (the S90 is an admired Japanese motorbike) which after a time becomes part of the sound structure and therefore meaning of the poem.[49] On the page, Smith's *Lawwwwwwwwd* is the S90. He also, like Big Yout and Sparrow and Miss Lou, uses ring-game refrain and proverb as reverb/eration with again amen and amen to the pentameter/computer.

> *Mi sey mi cyaaan believe it*
> *mi sey mi cyaaan believe it*
>
> room dem a rent
> mi apply widin
> but as mi go in
> cockroach an scarpian also come in
>
> *an mi cyaaan believe it*
>
> one likkle bwoy come blow im orn
> an mi look pan im wid scorn
> an mi realize ow mi fine bwoy pickney
> was a victim a de trix
> dem kell partisan pally-trix
> *an mi ban mi belly an mi baaal*
> *an mi ban mi belly an mi baaal*
> *lawwwwwd*
> *mi cyaaan believe it*

Mi dawta bwoyfren name is sailor
an im pass trew de port like a ship
more gran pickney fi feed
but de whole a wi need
wat a night wat a plight an we cyaan get a bite/mi life is a stiff fite

an mi cyaaan believe it . . .

> *Hi bwoy*
> yes mam
> *Hi bwoy*
> yes mam
> *Yu clean up de dwag shit?*
> yes mam
> *an mi cyaaan believe it*

Doris a moder a four
get a wuk as a domestic
boss man move in
an baps si sicai she pregnant again
baps si sicai an she pregnant again
an mi cyaaan believe it...

lawwwwwwwwwd...

but mi know yu believe it
lawwwwwwwwwwwwwwwd
mi know you believe it...[50]

A full presentation of nation language would, of course, include more traditional (ancestral/oral) material (e.g., shango,
anansesem, Spiritual [Aladura] Baptist services, grounnations,
yard theatres, ring games, tea-meeting speeches, etc, none of
which I've included here) as well as the extended performances
by Malik, Paul Keens-Douglas and the Barbados Writers Work-
shop, and others. In addition to the influence of Caribbean music
on Caribbean poetry, there has also been that of jazz, for example, and the wonderful speech rhythm effects being achieved
in a formal context by Morris, Scott, and Derek Walcott.

O so yu is Walcott?
You is Roddy brother?
Teacher Alex son? [51]

And Tony McNeill's

Strange   my writing to you

Can I say a cliché

Never thought I would see the day when you would cut me   glimpsed
you in   should have said at   should have said near   a bank one day;
smiled; waved; and you cut me

Catherine   name from the north

· ·

Catherine   name like a fir

The leaves turn with a fine cadence   The dancers touch hands under
the elms

· ·

I cry to the stones because I am lonely, the girl said to the dark

Perhaps if I look through this file I will find her charred letter

Catherine and Natalie, moving

The most beauteous virgin weeps in the rain

Catherine   if I talked to a fern do you think it would answer   if
I stopped at your window that

Hyacinths   I dial a number   soft click

A thrush glides in slow circles over the brook

Catherine stands by the fence, watching a leopard

I call you from fire   in the white wheel

I give you the valley.[52]

NOTES

1. No one, as far as I know, has yet made a study of the impact of Asiatic language
structures on the contemporary languages of the Caribbean, and even the study of
the African impact is still in its infancy. For development of Anglophone Caribbean
culture, see Edward Kamau Brathwaite, *Contradictory Omens: Cultural Diversity and
Integration in the Caribbean* (Mona, Jamaica: Savacou Publications, 1974).

2. See Alan Lomax, "Africanisms in New World Negro Music: A Cantometric Analysis," in *Research and Resources of Haiti,* ed. Richard P. Schaedel (New York: Re-

search Institute for the Study of Man, 1969) and in *The Haitian Potential,* ed. Vera Rubin and Richard P. Schaedel (New York: Teachers College Press, 1975); Mervyn C. Alleyne, "The Linguistic Continuity of Africa in the Caribbean," *Black Academy Review* 1, no. 4 (Winter 1970): 3-16.

3. The Maroons were Africans and escaped slaves who, after running away or participating in successful rebellions, set up autonomous societies throughout plantation America in marginal and certainly inaccessible areas outside European influence. See Richard Price, ed., *Maroon Societies: Rebel Slave Communities in the Americas* (Garden City, New York: Anchor Books, 1973). Nanny of the Maroons, an ex-Ashanti (?) Queen Mother, is regarded as one of the greatest of the Jamaica freedom fighters. See Edward Kamau Brathwaite, *Wars of Respect: Nanny, Sam Sharpe, and the Struggle for People's Liberation* (Kingston, Jamaica: Agency for Public Information, 1977).

4. But see Anthony Hinkson's Barbados hurricane poem, "Janet," in his unpublished collection "Slavation" (Bridgetown, Barbados: unpublished, c. 1976).

5. I am indebted to Ann Walmsley, editor of the anthology *The Sun's Eye: West Indian Writing for Young Readers* (London: Longmans, Green & Co. Ltd., 1968), for this example. For experiences of teachers trying to cope with West Indian English in Britain, see Chris Searle, *The Forsaken Lover: White Words and Black People* (London: Routledge & Kegan Paul, 1972) and *Okike* 15 (August 1979).

6. Derek Walcott, "The Schooner *Flight,*" in *The Star-Apple Kingdom* (New York: Farrar, Straus and Giroux, 1979), p. 3. William Langland's prelude to *Piers the Plowman* is often softened into "In somer season, whan soft was the sonne / I shope me in shroudes as I shepe were," which places it closer to Walcott—and to the pentameter.

7. But see the paragraphs and notes that follow.

8. See, for example, Ruth Finnegan, *Oral Literature in Africa* (Oxford: Clarendon Press, 1970); idem, *Oral Poetry: Its Nature, Significance, and Social Context* (Cambridge: At the University Press, 1977); idem, ed., *Penguin Anthology of Oral Poetry* (Harmondsworth: Penguin, 1977); B. W. Andrzejewski and I. M. Lewis, *Somali Poetry: An Introduction* (Oxford: Clarendon Press, 1964,); Jan Vansina, *Oral Tradition: A Study in Historical Methodology,* trans. H. M. Wright (London: Routledge & Kegan Paul, 1965); S. A. Babalola, *The Content and Form of Yoruba Ijala* (Oxford: Clarendon Press, 1966); Ulli Beier, ed., *Yoruba Poetry: An Anthology of Traditional Poems* (Cambridge: At the University Press, 1970); Marshall McLuhan, *The Gutenberg Galaxy: The Making of Typographic Man* (Toronto: University of Toronto Press, 1962); J.H.K. Nketia, *Funeral Dirges of the Akan People* (Achimota: n.p., 1955); I. & P. Opie, *The Lore and Language of Schoolchildren* (Oxford: Clarendon Press, 1967); B. A. Ogot, *History of the Southern Lue* (Nairobi: East African Publishing House, 1967); Jerome Rothenberg, ed., *Technicians of the Sacred: A Range of Poetries from Africa, America, Asia, and Oceania* (New York: Doubleday & Co., Inc., 1968); Dennis Tedlock, *Finding the Centre: Narrative Poetry of the Zuni Indians* (New York: Dial Press, 1972); R. Egudu and D. Nwoga, *Ibgo Traditional Verse* (London: Heinemann Educational Books Ltd., 1973); and the wonderfully rich literature on black culture in the Americas.

9. Frank Collymore, *Notes for a Glossary of Words and Phrases of Barbadian Dialect* (Bridgetown, Barbados: Advocate Co., 1955); A. J. Seymour, *Dictionary of Guyanese Folklore* (Georgetown, Guyana: National History and Arts Council, 1975); John R. Rickford, ed., *A Festival of Guyanese Words: Papers on Various Aspects of Guyanese Vocabulary* (Georgetown, Guyana: University of Guyana [mimeographed],

1978); Mervyn Alleyne, "The Cultural Matrix of Caribbean Dialects" (unpublished paper, University of the West Indies, Mona, West Indies, n.d.); "What is 'Jamaican' in Our Language?" a review of F. G. Cassidy and R. B. LePage's *Dictionary* in *Sunday Gleaner*, 9 July 1967. See also Maureen Warner Lewis (sometimes Warner), "African Feasts in Trinidad," *ASAWI Bulletin* 4 (1971); idem, "Africans in 19th-Century Trinidad," *ASAWI Bulletin* 5 (1972) and 6 (1973); idem, "Trinidad Yoruba—Notes on Survival," *Caribbean Quarterly* 17 (1971); idem, *The Nkuyu: Spirit Messengers of the Kumina* (Mona, West Indies: Savacou Publications, 1977), also in *Savacou* 13 (1977); idem, *Notes to Masks* [a study of Edward Kamau Brathwaite's poem] (Benin City, Nigeria: Ethiopia Press, 1977). See also Edward Kamau Brathwaite, "Brother Mais," [a study of Roger Mais's novel, *Brother Man*] *Tapia* (27 October 1974), which in an earlier version is the "Introduction" to Roger Mais, *Brother Man* (London: Heinemann Educational Books Ltd., 1974); idem, "Jazz and the West Indian Novel," *Bim* 44–46 (1967–68); idem, "The African Presence in Caribbean Literature," *Daedalus* (Spring 1974), reprinted in *Slavery, Colonialism, and Racism,* ed. Sidney Mintz (New York: W. W. Norton and Co., 1974), and trans. into Spanish in *Africa en America Latina,* ed. Manuel Moreno Fraginals (Paris: UNESCO, 1977); idem, "Kumina: The Spirit of African Survival in Jamaica," *Jamaica Journal* 42 (1978), and (in an earlier version) in *The African Dispersal* (Brookline, Mass.: Afro-American Studies Program, Boston University, 1979).

10. Edouard Glissant, "Free and Forced Poetics," *Alcheringa* 2 (1976).

11. See Bruce St. John's Introduction to his "Bumbatuk" poems, *Revista de Letras* (Mayaguez: University of Puerto Rico, 1972).

12. Brathwaite, "Jazz and the West Indian Novel."

13. Extended versions of this lecture attempt to demonstrate the link between music and language structures: e.g., Edward Kamau Brathwaite and *kaiso, aladura, sookee,* sermon, post-bop; Shake Keane and jazz, *cadence* and *anansesem*; Kwesi Johnson and Oku Onoura and reggae/dub; Michael Smith and ring-game and drumbeat; Malik and worksong; Paul Keens-Douglas and *conte*; Louise Bennet (Miss Lou) and folksay and street shout; Bruce St John and litany. Recent developments in kaiso (Shadow/*Bass man,* Short Shirt/*Tourist Leggo,* Sparrow/*Music an Rhythm; How you Jammin So*) suggest even more complex sound/shape developments.

14. The calypso (kaiso) is well treated in historical and musicological perspective by J. D. Elder, *Evolution of the Traditional Calypso of Trinidad and Tobago: A Sociohistorical Analysis of Song-change* (Ann Arbor, Mich.: University Microfilms, 1967), and by Errol Hill, *The Trinidad Carnival* (Austin: University of Texas Press, 1972). But it is Gordon Rohlehr, a critic and reader in English at the University of the West Indies, who, apart from a few comments by C.L.R. James and Derek Walcott, is almost the only major Caribbean writer to have dealt with the literary aspects of kaiso, and with the relationship between kaiso (and reggae) and literature. Among Rohlehr's articles are: "Sparrow and the Language of Calypso," *CAM Newsletter* 2 (1967), and *Savacou* 2 (1970); "Calypso and Morality," *Moko* (17 June 1969); "The Calypso as Rebellion," *S.A.G.* 3 (1970); "Sounds and Pressure: Jamaican Blues," *Cipriani Labour College Review* (Jan. 1970); "Calypso and Politics," *Moko* (29 Oct. 1971); "Forty Years of Calypso," *Tapia* (3 and 17 Sept. 1972 and 8 Oct. 1972); "Samuel Selvon and the Language of the People," in Edward Baugh, ed., *Critics on Caribbean Literature* (London: George Allen & Unwin, 1978), pp. 153–61; and "The Folk in Caribbean Literature," *Tapia* (17 Dec. 1972).

15. See G. E. Simpson, *Religious Cults of the Caribbean* (Rio Piedras, Puerto Rico: Institute of Caribbean Studies of the University of Puerto Rico, 1970); Honor Ford-Smith, "The Performance Aspect of Kumina Ritual," Seminar Paper, Department of English, University of the West Indies, Mona, Jamaica (1976); and works by Brathwaite and Warner Lewis, as cited in note 9 above.

16. See Wayne F. Cooper, *The Passion of Claude McKay: Selected Poetry and Prose, 1912–1948* (New York: Schocken Books, 1973).

17. Claude McKay's first two books of poetry (1912), written in Jamaica, are unique in that they are the first all-dialect collections from an Anglophone Caribbean poet. They are, however, *dialect* as distinct from *nation* because McKay allowed himself to be imprisoned in the pentameter; he did not let his language find its own parameters, though this raises the tricky question of *critical relativity*. Could McKay, in the Jamaica of 1912, have done it any different—with a svengali like Walter Jekyll, for instance, plus his *Dan-is-the-man-in-the-van* schoolteacher brother? We can certainly note the results of his literary colonialism in the primordial (?) anglicanism of *Constab Ballads* (London: Watts, 1912) and *Songs of Jamaica* (Kingston, Jamaica: Aston W. Gardner, 1912):

> I've a longin' in me dept's of heart
> > dat I can conquer not,
> 'Tis a wish dat I've been havin' from since
> > I could form a t'o't,
> Just to view de homeland England, in de streets of London walk
> An' to see de famous sights dem
> > 'bouten which dere's so much talk . . .

> > > ("Old England," *Songs,* p. 63)

By the time we reach Louise Bennet in the forties there is much less of a problem. Although the restrictive forms are still there, there is a world of difference in the activity of the language, and one suspects that this very restriction (the formal meter) is used as an aid to memory in performance. Many less adventurous spirits in the fifties attempted dialect in their first editions but revised them upward in subsequent versions. We are fortunate to have for purposes of comparison, in N. R. Millington's *Lingering Thoughts* (Bridgetown, Barbados: privately published, 1954), two versions of "On Return from a Foreign Land" (the dialect is entirely absent from subsequent editions):

Oh, what a rare delight	"Who you and whay you come from?
To see you once again!	Yuh voice soun' Bajun
Your kindly, strong, familiar face	An' yuh face familiuh.
Comes easily to my remembrance.	Las' time I see yuh was 'pon Roebuck
Our last meeting was on Roebuck	Street,
Street	Dat use' to be suh full o' holes
which used to be so rutty.	But now un hear dat all de roads been
The mule-drawn car is gone;	tar
Gone, too, the railway;	De tramcars gone, de train gone too
Running on the tarmac	An' buses runnin' everywhay
Are the fussy buses.	At any owuh o' de day.

Small estates are combining into large . . .	De little estates all shut down, An' everybody rush to town . . ."
(p. 40)	(p. 43)

Two more points are that Millington places the dialect version in quotes to signal (for him) its dramatic/conversational mode; and, at a reading of this poem by the author in 1979, he removed the awkward standard English "rutty" and imported from the dialect version the more natural "full of holes."

18. Claude McKay, "St Issac's Church, Petrograd," first published in *Survey Graphic* 53 (1925), and subsequently in *Selected Poems of Claude McKay* (New York: Bookman Associates, 1953), p. 84, and in Cooper, ed., *Passion of Claude McKay*, p. 127; it was also read and recorded by the author in Arna Bontemps, ed., *Anthology of Negro Poets* (New York: Folkways Records, FL 9791, 1966).

19. George Campbell, "On this Night," in *First Poems* (Kingston, Jamaica: privately published, 1945), p. 67.

20. See the discussion of the issue of McKay and *critical relativity* in note 17, above.

21. The tape recordings used in this lecture were taken from a wide variety of sources: long-playing albums (LPs), field recordings, copies from radio broadcasts, interviews, etc. The Lamming recording is from one of our finest radio programs, *New World of the Caribbean,* a series sponsored by Bookers of Guyana and broadcast on Radio Guyana in 1955-56. It was conceived and written by Lamming and Wilson Harris and produced for radio by Rafiq Khan. The Lamming reading of Campbell's poem had as background the theme music of the entire series, Dvořák's *New World* Symphony.

22. The Mighty Sparrow (Slinger Francisco), "Dan is the man in the van," on an EP (extended play, 45 rpm) recording (Port of Spain, Trinidad: National Recording Co., 1958?). The fourth line of each quatrain, shouted by Sparrow on this recording, represents the "response" part of this form and is sometimes sung by chorus and/or audience. For the text of this kaiso, see *One Hundred and Twenty Calypsoes to Remember . . . by the Mighty Sparrow* (Port of Spain, Trinidad: National Recording Co., 1963), p. 86.

23. The Mighty Sparrow, "Ten to One Is Murder" (EP recording) (Port of Spain, Trinidad, National Recording Co., 1960). For the text see *One Hundred and Twenty Calypsoes,* p. 37.

24. For the role of color in the Caribbean, see Fernando Henriques, *Family and Colour in Jamaica* (London: Eyre & Spottiswoode, 1953).

25. See the Ph.D. dissertation (in progress) by Mary Jane Hewitt (Department of English and History, University of the West Indies, Mona, Jamaica), on Louise Bennett and Zora Neale Hurston as "cultural conservators."

26. ACLALS (Association of Commonwealth Literature and Language Societies) Conference held at the University of the West Indies, Mona, Jamaica, in January 1971; see Edward Kamau Brathwaite, "The Love Axe/l: Developing a Caribbean Aesthetic," in *Reading Black: Essays in the Criticism of African, Caribbean, and Black American Literature,* ed. Houston A. Baker, Jr. (Ithaca, N.Y.: Cornell University Press, 1976), pp. 20-36; also published in *Bim* 61-63 (1977-78).

27. McKay's relationship with Jekyll is recorded in McKay's autobiography, *My Green Hills of Jamaica* (Kingston, Jamaica: Heinemann Educational Books [Carib-

bean] Ltd., 1979), pp. 65-72, 76-79. For a useful note on Jekyll, see Cooper, *Passion of Claude McKay*, pp. 318-19.

28. Ms. Bennett's first book of poetry, *Dialect Verses*, was printed for the author in Kingston, Jamaica, by the Gleaner Co. in 1940—five years before the editor of the *Gleaner* recognized her.

29. Louise Bennett, *Caribbean Quarterly* 4, nos. 1 and 2 (March-June 1968): 98.

30. Federal 204, Federal Records, Kingston, Jamaica, 1967.

31. Personal communication, Louise Bennett Coverley (25 Sept. 1978).

32. Louise Bennett, "Pedestrian Crosses," in *Jamaica Labrish* (Kingston, Jamaica: Sangster's Book Stores Jamaica, 1966), p. 74.

33. Louise Bennett, "Dutty tough," in *Jamaica Labrish*, pp. 120-21. The tyranny of the pentameter can be seen/heard quite clearly here, although Miss Lou erodes and transforms this with the sound of her language. Its "riddim" sets up a counterpoint *against* the pentameter: "River flood but water scarce/yaw; yuh noh se/Cyar an truck *backa me*." The Africanisms *koo de, galang, yah, yaw, noh nuff, deh dahblow*, and *fe*, for example, carry this even further, crystallizing in brilliant roots images such as "like fat is sin" and "tun dumplin refugee," which not only has its English meaning, but its folk-speech underdrone of African sound words for food: *tun, tum, tuntum*, and *fungee*. A whole essay could (and should) be written on the phonemic structure of nation language and how this relates to syntax and prosody, in addition to the historical and critical/comparative approaches hinted at in note 17 of this study.

34. For those of us who really made the breakthrough, it was Eliot's actual voice—or rather his recorded voice, property of the British Council (Barbados)—reading "Preludes," "The Love Song of J. Alfred Prufrock," *The Waste Land*, and later the *Four Quartets*—not the texts—which turned us on. In that dry deadpan delivery, the "riddims" of St. Louis (though we did not know the source then) were stark and clear for those of us who at the same time were listening to the dislocations of Bird, Dizzy, and Klook. And it is interesting that, on the whole, the establishment could not stand Eliot's voice—and far less jazz. Another influence must have been the voice of John Arlott, the British Broadcasting Corporation (BBC) test cricket commentator, who stunned, amazed, and transported us with his natural, "riddimic" and image laden tropes in his revolutionary Hampshire burr, at a time when BBC meant Empire and Loyal Models and Our Master's voice, and cricket, especially against England, was the national sport—our solitary occasions for communal catharsis one way or the other. Not only was Arlott "good" (all our mimics tried to imitate him), but he subverted the establishment with the way he spoke and where: like Eliot, like jazz . . .

35. H. A. Vaughan, "For certain demagogues," read by the author on the recording, *Poets of the West Indies Reading Their Own Works* (New York: Caedmon TC 1379, 1971), and printed in *Sandy Lane and Other Poems* (Bridgetown, Barbados: privately published by author, 1945), and in *Caribbean Voices: An Anthology of West Indian Poetry*, ed. John Figueroa (London: Evans Brothers Ltd., 1970), pp. 71-72. By *cobblers* Vaughan does not mean ye old English shoemakers, but (scavenger) seabirds (*corbeaux*). Vaughan's reading of the italicized stanza is especially interesting.

36. Frank Collymore died in July 1980, while this edition of my talk was being prepared. I should like here to pay tribute to his warmth, kindness, and humanity, and to his enormous contribution to Caribbean literature.

37. Frank Collymore, "Voici la Plume de mon Oncle," in his *Collected Poems* (Bridgetown, Barbados: privately published, 1959), p. 92; read by the author on the *Poets of the West Indies* recording.

38. Edward Kamau Brathwaite, "Wings of a Dove," in his *Rights of Passage* (London: Oxford University Press, 1967), p. 44; also printed in his *The Arrivants: A New World Trilogy* (London: Oxford University Press, 1973), p. 45; and read by the author on the recordings *Rights of Passage* (London: Argo Records, Argo DA 101 and DA 102, 1969; repressed on DA 1110 and DA 1111, 1972).

39. Linton Kwesi Johnson, "Five Nights of Bleeding," on the LP recording *Dread Beat an' Blood* (London: Virgin Records, FL 1017, 1978); for text see *Dread Beat and Blood* (London: Bogle-L'Ouverture Publications Ltd., 1975), pp. 15–16.

40. Edward Kamau Brathwaite, "The Dust," in *Rights of Passage,* pp. 66–67, and in *The Arrivants,* pp. 65–66; read by the author on the Argo 102 and 1111 recordings.

41. Bongo Jerry, *Savacou* 3/4 (1970/1971), pp. 13–15. At the Harvard lecture, a tape recording of Bongo Jerry reading his poem, with *funde* and *repeater* drums, at a rasta *grounnation* (Kingston, 1969) was used; also Jerry's slide trombone tribute to Don Drummond, Bob Marley's musical and spiritual ancestor. The influence of this *roots underground* is described in Brathwaite, "Love Axe/l."

42. John Figueroa, "Portrait of a Woman," *Savacou* 3/4 (1970/1971), pp. 138–39; read by the author on the recording *Poets of the West Indies.*

43. Derek Walcott, "Blues," in his *The Gulf and Other Poems* (London: Jonathan Cape, 1969); also found in *The Gulf* (New York: Farrar, Straus & Giroux, 1970), p. 67; read by the author on the recording *Poetry International '69,* ed. Peter Orr (London: Argo Records, MPR 262 and 263, 1970). In my presentation, Walcott's reading was followed by Don Drummond's "Green Island" solo from the LP recording *In Memory of Don Drummond* (Kingston, Jamaica: Studio One, 1965?).

44. The premiere of the Jimmy Cliff roots/reggae film, *The Harder They Come* (Kingston, Jamaica: Perry Henzell, 1972), marked a dislocation of the sociocolonial pentameter in the same way that its music, and its stars, and their style marked a revolution in the hierarchical structure in the arts of the Caribbean. At the premiere, the traditional "order of service" was reversed. Instead of the elite moving from their cars into the Carib Cinema, watched by the poor and admiring multitude, the multitude took over—the car park, the steps, the barred gates, the magical lantern itself—and demanded they they see what they had wrought. "For the first time at last" it was the people (the raw material), not the critics, who decided the criteria of praise, the measure and grounds of qualification; "for the first time at last," a local face, a native icon, a nation language voice was hero. In this small corner of our world, a revolution was as significant as emancipation.

45. Walcott, "Blues" (New York ed.), p. 68; and on the *Poetry International* recording.

46. Exile is the first significant feature of Anglophone Caribbean writing: it is the need—or the imagined need—to emigrate to metropolitan centers in order to exist as writers. Our native literature begins with McKay the exile (see his *Home to Harlem* [New York: Harper & Brothers, 1928]); and it is ending its first phase with Lammig, *Pleasures of Exile* and V. S. Naipaul (see *Newsweek,* 18 August 1980).

47. Mrs. Imogene Elizabeth Kennedy (Miss Queenie), tape recorded conversation with Maureen Warner Lewis and Monica Schuler (Kingston, Jamaica, June 1971). See Brathwaite, "Kumina," pp. 45–63; and Warner Lewis, *The Nkuyu.*

48. All of Kwesi Johnson's LP recordings to date—*Dread Beat an' Blood* (1978), *Forces of Victory* (1979), *Bass Culture* (1980)—have been on the British reggae charts. *Bass Culture* was ranked number 3 in June 1980 (see *Black Music and Jazz Review* [June 1980], p. 12). Oku Onoura has performed with Bob Marley; Paul Keens-Douglas with The Mighty Sparrow and with Miss Lou; Brathwaite with the Mystic Revelation of Rastafari and with Light of Saba; Michael Smith with Light of Saba (on the recording *Word Sound* [Kingston, Jamaica: Light of Saba 002, 1978]); and Malik (of Trinidad) has presented several elaborate concerts with his own musicians. For more on these developments, see Edward Kamau Brathwaite, "Explosion of Caribbean Sound Poetry," *Caribbean Contact* (1978), p. 9.

49. The concept of *noise* as part of the music of the oral tradition has pervaded (for several reasons) this presentation. I am indebted to Kwabena Nketia for clarifying for me the idea. Noise is that decorative energy that invests the nation performance. Unnecessary but without which not enough. Whistlee, grater, scraper, shak-shak, shekesheke, wood block, gong gong, the cheng-cheng of the steel band, the buzz of the banjo or cymbal, the grrill of the guitar, vibrato of voice, sax, sound system, the long roll of the drum until it becomes noise, Coltrane sheets of sound, Pharoah Sander's honks and cries, onomatopoeia, congregational kinesis . . .

50. Michael Smith, "Mi Cyaaan Believe It," on *Word Sound,* with written version from draft by Smith and transcription by Brathwaite, in Edward Kamau Brathwaite, ed., *New Poets from Jamaica, Savacou* 14/15 (1979): 84–86.

51. Derek Walcott, "Sainte Lucia," in his *Sea Grapes* (London: Jonathan Cape, 1976), p. 46.

52. Anthony McNeill, *Credences at the Altar of Cloud* (Kingston, Jamaica: Institute of Jamaica, 1979), pp. 134–35.

Leslie Marmon Silko

Language and Literature
from a Pueblo Indian Perspective

Where I come from, the words that are most highly valued are those which are spoken from the heart, unpremeditated and unrehearsed. Among the Pueblo people, a written speech or statement is highly suspect because the true feelings of the speaker remain hidden as he reads words that are detached from the occasion and the audience. I have intentionally not written a formal paper to read to this session because of this and because I want you to hear and to experience Enlish in a nontraditional structure, a structure that follows patterns from the oral tradition. For those of you accustomed to a structure that moves from point A to point B to point C, this presentation may be somewhat difficult to follow because the structure of Pueblo expression resembles something like a spider's web—with many little threads radiating from a center, criss-crossing each other. As with the web, the structure will emerge as it is made and you must simply listen and trust, as the Pueblo people do, that meaning will be made.

I suppose the task that I have today is a formidable one because basically I come here to ask you, at least for a while, to set aside a number of basic approaches that you have been using and probably will continue to use in approaching the study of English or the study of language; first of all, I come to ask you to see language from the Pueblo perspective, which is a perspective that is very much concerned with including the whole of creation and the whole of history and time. And so we very seldom talk about breaking language down into

---

This "essay" is an edited transcript of an oral presentation. The "author" deliberately did not read from a prepared paper so that the audience could experience firsthand one dimension of the oral tradition—non-linear structure. Her remarks were intended to be heard, not read.

words. As I will continue to relate to you, even the use of a specific language is less important than the one thing—which is the "telling," or the storytelling. And so, as Simon Ortiz has written, if you approach a Pueblo person and want to talk words or, worse than that, to break down an individual word into its components, ofttimes you will just get a blank stare, because we don't think of words as being isolated from the speaker, which, of course, is one element of the oral tradition. Moreover, we don't think of words as being alone: words are always with other words, and the other words are almost always in a story of some sort.

Today I have brought a number of examples of stories in English because I would like to get around to the question that has been raised, or the topic that has come along here, which is what changes we Pueblo writers might make with English as a language for literature. But at the same time I would like to explain the importance of storytelling and how it relates to a Pueblo theory of language.

So first I would like to go back to the Pueblo Creation story. The reason I go back to that story is because it is an all-inclusive story of creation and how life began. Tséitsínako, Thought Woman, by thinking of her sisters, and together with her sisters, thought of everything which is, and this world was created. And the belief was that everything in this world was a part of the original creation, and that the people at home realized that far away there were others—other human beings. There is even a section of the story which is a prophesy—which describes the origin of the European race, the African, and also remembers the Asian origins.

Starting out with this story, with this attitude which includes all things, I would like to point out that the reason the people are more concerned with story and communication and less with a particular language is in part an outgrowth of the area [pointing to a map] where we find ourselves. Among the twenty Pueblos there are at least six distinct languages, and possibly

seven. Some of the linguists argue—and I don't set myself up to
be a linguist at all—about the number of distinct languages. But
certainly Zuni is all alone, and Hopi is all alone, and from mesa
to mesa there are subtle differences in language—very great differences. I think that this might be the reason that what particular language was being used wasn't as important as what a
speaker was trying to say. And this, I think, is reflected and
stems or grows out of a particular view of the story—that is,
that language *is* story. At Laguna many words have stories
which make them. So when one is telling a story, and one is
using words to tell the story, each word that one is speaking
has a story of its own too. Often the speakers or tellers go into
the stories of the words they are using to tell one story so that
you get stories within stories, so to speak. This structure becomes very apparent in the storytelling, and what I would like
to show you later on by reading some pieces that I brought is
that this structure also informs the writing and the stories which
are currently coming from Pueblo people. I think what is essential is this sense of story, and story within story, and the idea
that one story is only the beginning of many stories, and the
sense that stories never truly end. I would like to propose that
these views of structure and the dynamics of storytelling are
some of the contributions which Native American cultures
bring to the English language or at least to literature in the English language.

   First of all, a lot of people think of storytelling as something
that is done at bedtime—that it is something that is done for
small children. When I use the term storytelling, I include a far
wider range of telling activity. I also do not limit storytelling to
simply old stories, but to again go back to the original view of
creation, which sees that it is all part of a whole; we do not dif-
ferentiate or fragment stories and experiences. In the beginning,
Tséitsínako, Thought Woman, thought of all these things, and
all of these things are held together as one holds many things
together in a single thought.

So in the telling (and today you will hear a few of the dimensions of this telling) first of all, as was pointed out earlier, the storytelling always includes the audience and the listeners, and, in fact, a great deal of the story is believed to be inside the listener, and the storyteller's role is to draw the story out of the listeners. This kind of shared experience grows out of a strong community base. The storytelling goes on and continues from generation to generation.

The Origin story functions basically as a maker of our identity—with the story we know who we are. We are the Lagunas. This is where we came from. We came this way. We came by this place. And so from the time you are very young, you hear these stories, so that when you go out into the wider world, when one asks who you are, or where are you from, you immediately know: we are the people who came down from the north. We are the people of these stories. It continues down into clans so that you are not just talking about Laguna Pueblo people, you are talking about your own clan. Within the clans there are stories which identify the clan.

In the Creation story, Antelope says that he will help knock a hole in the earth so that the people can come up, out into the next world. Antelope tries and tries, and he uses his hooves and is unable to break through; and it is then that Badger says, "Let me help you." And Badger very patiently uses his claws and digs a way through, bringing the people into the world. When the Badger clan people think of themselves, or when the Antelope people think of themselves, it is as people who are of *this* story, and this is *our* place, and we fit into the very beginning when the people first came, before we began our journey south.

So you can move, then, from the idea of one's identity as a tribal person into clan identity. Then we begin to get to the extended family, and this is where we begin to get a kind of story coming into play which some people might see as a different kind of story, though Pueblo people do not. Anthropologists and ethnologists have, for a long time, differentiated the types of oral language they find in the Pueblos. They tended to rule out all but the old and sacred and traditional stories and were not interested in family stories and the family's account of itself. But these family stories are just as important as the other stories—the older stories. These family stories are given equal recognition. There is no definite, pre-set pattern for the way one will hear the stories of one's own family, but it is a very critical part of one's childhood, and it continues on throughout one's life. You will hear stories of importance to the family— sometimes wonderful stories—stories about the time a maternal uncle got the biggest deer that was ever seen and brought back from the mountains. And so one's sense of who the family is, and who you are, will then extend from that—"I am from the family of my uncle who brought in this wonderful deer, and it was a wonderful hunt"—so you have this sort of building or sense of identity.

There are also other stories, stories about the time when another uncle, perhaps, did something that wasn't really acceptable. In other words, this process of keeping track, of telling, is an all-inclusive process which begins to create a total picture. So it is very important that you know all of the stories—both positive and not so positive—about one's own family. The reason that it is very important to keep track of all the stories in one's own family is because you are liable to hear a story from somebody else who is perhaps an enemy of the family, and you are liable to hear a version which has been changed, a version which makes your family sound disreputable—something that will taint the honor of the family. But if you have already heard the story, you know your family's version of what *really* happened that night, so when somebody else is mentioning it, you will have a version of the story to counterbalance it. Even when there is no way around it—old Uncle Pete did a terrible thing— by knowing the stories that come out of other families, by keeping very close watch, listening constantly to learn the stories about other families, one is in a sense able to deal with terrible sorts of things that might happen within one's own family. When a member of one's own family does something that cannot be excused, one always knows stories about similar things which happened in other families. And it is not done maliciously. I think it is very important to realize this. Keeping track of all the stories within the community gives a certain distance, a useful perspective which brings incidents down to a level we can deal with. If others have done it before, it cannot be so terrible. If others have endured, so can we.

The stories are always bringing us together, keeping this whole together, keeping this family together, keeping this clan together. "Don't go away, don't isolate yourself, but come here, because we have all had these kinds of experiences"—this is what the people are saying to you when they tell you these other stories. And so there is this constant pulling together to resist what seems to me to be a basic part of human nature: when some violent emotional experience takes place, people get the urge to run off and hide or separate themselves from others. And of course, if we do that, we are not only talking about endangering the group, we are also talking about the individual or the individual family never being able to recover or to survive. Inherent in this belief is the feeling that one does not recover or get well by one's self, but it is together that we look after each other and take care of each other.

In the storytelling, then, we see this process of bringing people together, and it works not only on the family level, but also on the level of the individual. Of course, the whole Pueblo concept of the individual is a little bit different from the usual Western concept of the individual. But one of the beauties of the storytelling is that when something happens to an individual, many people will come to you and take you aside, or maybe a couple of people will come and talk to you. These are occasions of storytelling. These occasions of storytelling are continuous; they are a way of life.

Storytelling lies at the heart of the Pueblo people, and so when someone comes in and says, "When did they tell the stories, or what time of day does the storytelling take place?" that is a ridiculous question. The storytelling goes on constantly—as some old grandmother puts on the shoes of a little child and tells the child the story of a little girl who didn't wear her shoes. At the same time somebody comes into the house for coffee to talk with an adolescent boy who has just been into a lot of trouble, to reassure him that *he* got into that kind of trouble, or somebody else's son got into that kind of trouble too. You have this constant ongoing process, working on many different levels.

One of the stories I like to bring up about helping the individual in crisis is a recent story, and I want to remind you that we make no distinctions between the stories—whether they are history, whether they are fact, whether they are gossip—these distinctions are not useful when we are talking about this particular experience with language. Anyway, there was a young man who, when he came back from the war in Vietnam, had saved up his Army pay and bought a beautiful red Volkswagen Beetle. He was very proud of it, and one night drove up to a place right across the reservation line. It is a very notorious place for many reasons, but one of the more notorious things about the place is a deep arroyo behind the place. This is the King's Bar. So he ran in to pick up a cold six-pack to take home, but he didn't put on his emergency brake. And his little red Volkswagen rolled back into the arroyo and was all smashed up. He felt very bad about it, but within a few days everybody had come to him and told him stories about other people who had lost cars to that arroyo. And probably the story that made him feel the best was about the time that George Day's station wagon, with his mother-in-law and kids in the back, rolled into that arroyo. So everybody was saying, "Well, at least your mother-in-law and kids weren't in the car when it rolled in," and you can't argue with that kind of story. He felt better then because he wasn't alone anymore. He and his smashed-up Volks-wagen were now joined with all the other stories of cars that fell into that arroyo.

Again there is a very beautiful little story. It comes from far out of the past. It is a story that is sometimes told to people who suffer great family or personal loss. I would like to read that story to you now, and while I am reading it to you, try to listen on a couple of levels at once. I want you to listen to the usage of English. I came from a family which has been doing something that isn't exactly standard English for a while. I come from a family which, basically, is intent on getting the stories told; and we *will* get those stories told, and language *will* work for us. It is imperative to tell and not to worry over a specific language. The imperative is the telling. This is an old story from Aunt Suzie. She is one of the first generations of persons at Laguna who began experimenting with our notion of English—who began working to make English speak for us—that is, to speak from the heart. As I read the story to you, you will hear some words that came from Carlisle. She was taken from Laguna, New Mexico, on a train when she was a little girl, and she spent six years at Carlisle, Pennsylvania, in an Indian school, which was like being sent to prison. But listen and you will hear the Carlisle influence. This is a story that is sometimes given to you when there has been a great loss.

> This took place partly in old Acoma and Laguna. Waithia was a little girl living in Acoma. One day she said, "Mother, I would like to have some yastoah to eat." Yastoah is the hardened crust of corn meal mush that curls up. The very name *yastoah* means sort of "curled up," you know, dried, just as mush dries on top. She said, "I would like to have some yastoah," and her mother said, "My dear little girl, I can't make you any yastoah because we haven't any wood, but if you will go down off the mesa, down below, and pick up some pieces of wood, bring them home and I will make you some yastoah." So Waithia was glad and ran down the precipitous cliff of the mesa. Down below, just as her mother told her, there were pieces of wood, some curled, some crooked in shape, that she was to pick up and take home. She found just such wood as these.

She went home and she had them in a little wickerlike bag. First she called to her mother as she got home and said, "Mother, upstairs." The Pueblo people always called "upstairs" because long ago their homes were two or three stories, and that was their entrance, from the top. She said, "*Naya, deeni!* Mother, upstairs!" And her mother came. The little girl said, "I have brought the wood you wanted me to bring." She opened her little wicker basket and laid them out and they were snakes. They were snakes instead of the crooked pieces of wood, and her mother said, "Oh, my dear child. You have brought snakes instead." She says, "Go take them back and put them back just where you got them." The little girl ran down the mesa again. Down below to the flats. And she put those snakes back just where she got them. They were snakes instead, and she was very much hurt about this, and she said, "I am not going home. I am going away to the beautiful lake place and drown myself in that lake, Kawaik *bunyanah*, to the west. I will go there and drown myself."

So she started off, and as she came by the Enchanted Mesa, Kátsima, she met an old man, very aged, and he saw her running, and he said, "My dear child, where are you going?" She said, "I am going to Kawaik and jump into the lake there." "Why?" "Well, because," she says, "my mother didn't want to make any yastoah." And the old man said, "Oh, no, you must not go my child. Come with me and I will take you home." He tried to catch her, but she was very light and skipped along, and every time he would try to grab her she would skip faster away from him.

So he was coming home with some wood on his back, strapped to his back and tied with yucca. He just let that strap go and let the wood fall. He went as fast as he could up the cliff to the little girl's home. When he got to the place where she lived, he called to her mother, "*Deeni!* Upstairs!" "Come on up." And he says, "I can't. I just came to bring you a message. Your little daughter is running away. She is going to Kawaik to drown herself in the lake there." "Oh, my dear little girl!" the mother said. So she busied herself around and made her the yastoah she loved so much. Corn mush, curled at the top. She must have found enough wood to boil the corn meal and make the yastoah.

And while the mush was cooling, she got the little girl's clothing, she got the little dress and all her other garments, little buckskin moccasins that she had, and put them in a bundle, too—probably a yucca bag. And she started down as fast as she could on the east side of Acoma. There used to be a trail there, you know. It's gone now. But it was accessible in those days. And she followed, and she saw her way at a distance—saw the daughter—she kept calling: "Tsumatusu, my daughter, come back. I have got your yastoah for you." But the little girl did not turn. She kept on ahead, and she cried. And what she cried is the song: "My mother, my mother, she didn't want me to have any yastoah. So now I am going to go away and drown myself." Her mother heard her cry and said, "My little daughter, come back here." "No," and she kept a distance away from her.

And they came nearer and nearer to the lake that was here. And she could see her daughter now, very plain. "Come back, my daughter, I have your yastoah." And no, she kept on, and finally she reached the lake, and she stood on the edge. She tied a little feather in her hair, which is traditional: in death they tie this little feather on the head. She carried a little feather, the girl did, and she tied it in her hair with a little piece of string, right on top of her head she put the feather. Just about as her mother was to reach her, she jumped into the lake. The little feather was whirling around and around in the depths below.

Of course the mother was very sad. She went, grieved, back to Acoma and climbed her mesa home, and the little clothing, the little moccasins she brought, and the yastoah. She stood on the edge of the mesa and scattered them out. She scattered them to the east and west, to the north and to the south—in all directions and where every one of the little clothing and the little moccasins and shawls and yastoah, all of them turned into butterflies, all colors of butterflies! And today they say that Acoma has more beautiful butterflies: red ones, white ones, blue ones, yellow ones. They came from this little girl's clothing.*

Now that is a story that anthropologists would consider to be a very old story. The version I have given you is just as Aunt Suzie tells it. You can occasionally hear some English she picked up at Carlisle—words like "precipitous." You will also notice that there is a great deal of repetition, and a little reminder about yastoah and how it was made. There is a remark about the cliff trail at Acoma—that it was once there, but is there no longer. This story may be told at a time of sadness or loss, but within this story many other elements are brought together. Things are not separated out and put into separate categories; all things are brought together. So that the reminder about the yastoah is valuable information that is repeated, a recipe, if you will. The information about the old trail at Acoma reveals that stories are, in a sense, maps, since even to this day there is little information or material about trails that is passed around with writing. In the structure of this story the repetitions are, of course, designed to help you be able to remember. It is repeated again and again, and then it moves on. There is a very definite pattern that you will hear in these pieces.

The next story that I would like to read to you is by Simon Ortiz from Acoma Pueblo. He is a wonderful poet and works also in narrative, and one of the things that I find in this piece of short fiction to be very interesting is that if you listen very closely, you begin to hear what I was talking about in terms of a story never beginning at the beginning. And they certainly never end. As the Hopis sometimes say, "Well, it has gone this far for a while." But there is always that implication of a continuing. The other thing that I want you to listen for is within one story there are many other stories together again. There is always, *always* this dynamic of bringing things together, of interrelating things. It is an imperative in Pueblo oral literature, it seems to me, and it occurs structurally in narrative and in fiction. Listen to the kinds of stories contained within the main story. Through the narrative you can begin to see a family identity and an individual identity, while at the same time it addresses a particular incident. "It was that time. . . ." Listen to this and see if you can hear these things. This is called "Home Country," a short piece that Simon Ortiz has recently completed:

> Well, it's been a while. I think in 1947 was when I left. My husband had been killed in Okinawa some years before and so I had no more husband, and I had to make a living. Oh, I guess I could have looked for another man, but I didn't want to. It looked like the war had made them into a bad way. I saw some of them come home like that. They either got drunk or just stayed around a while or couldn't seem to be

satisfied any more with what was there at home. I guess now that I
think about it, that happened to me too, although I wasn't in the war,
in the army, or even much off the reservation; just those years at Indian school. Well, there was that feeling, things were changing not only
the men and the boys, but things were changing. One day the home
nurse, the nurse that came from the Indian health service was at my
mother's home. My mother was getting near the end, real sick; and she
said that she had been meaning to ask me a question. I said, "What is the
question?" And the home nurse said, "Well, your mother is getting real
sick and after she is no longer around for you to take care of, what will
you be doing? You and her are the only ones here." And I said, "I
don't know." But I was thinking about it. What she said made me think
about it. And the next time she came she said, "Eloise, the government
is hiring Indians now in the Indian schools to take care of the boys and
girls. I heard one of the supervisors say that Indians are hard workers,
but you have to supervise them a lot. And I thought of you. Well, because you have been taking care of your mother real good and you follow all my instructions." She said, "I thought of you because you are a
good Indian girl and you would be the kind of person for that job." I
didn't say anything. I had not even thought about a job, but I kept
thinking about it.

Well, my mother died and we buried her up on the cemetery. It is
real nice on the east side of the hill, where the sun shines and the wind
doesn't blow too much sand around right there. Well, I was sad. We
were all sad for a while, but, you know how things are. One of my
auntys came in and advised me and warned me about being too sad
about the end. She wished me that I would not worry too much about
it because old folks go along pretty soon. Life is that way and then she
said maybe I ought to take in one of my aunty's kids or two because
there was a lot of them kids and I was all by myself now. But I was so
young and I thought that I might do that, you know, take care of someone. But I had been thinking too, about what the home nurse had said
to me about working. Hardly anybody at our home was working at
something like that. No woman, anyway. And I would have to move
away.

Well, I did just that. I remember that day very well. I thought my
auntys and we were all crying and we all went up to the highway where
the bus to town passes by every day. I was wearing an old kind of bluish sweater that was kind of bluish, that one of my cousins had got
from a white person—a tourist one summer—in trade for something she
had made, a real pretty basket. She gave me that and I used to have a

picture of me with it on. It's kind of real ugly. Yeah, that was the day I left wearing a baggy sweater, carrying a suitcase that someone gave me, too. Well, I think, or maybe it was the home nurse. There wasn't much in it, either. I was scared and everyone seemed to be sad. I was young and skinny then. My aunt said (one of them who was real fat), "You make sure you eat now. Make your own tortillas, drink milk and stuff like candy is not good." She learned that from the nurse. "Make sure you got your letter, honey," and I said I had it folded in my purse. Yes, I had one purse, a brown one of my husband's when he was still alive and home on furlough. He bought it on my birthday. It was a nice purse and still looked new because I never used it. The letter said I had a job at Keams Canyon, at the boarding school there. But I would have to go to the Agency first for some papers to be filled. And that's where I was going first, the Agency. And then they would send me out to Keams Canyon. I didn't even know where it was except that one of our relatives said that it was near Hopi. My uncles teased me about watching out for the Hopi men and boys. Don't let them get too close, they said. You know how they are—they're pretty strict about those things. And they were joking, and they really weren't joking. And so I said, "Oh, they won't get near me. I'm too ugly." And I promised I would be careful anyway.

So we all gathered for a while at my last aunty's house, and then the old man, my grandfather brought his horses and wagon to the door. We all got in and sat there for a while until my aunty called her father: "Okay, father, let's go," and shook his elbow because the old man was old by then and kind of going to sleep all the time. You had to talk to him real loud. I had about $10.00, I think. That was a lot of money; more than it is now, you know. And while we got to the highway where the Indian road, which is just a dirt road, goes off the paved road, my grandfather reached into his blue jeans and pulled out a silver dollar and put it into my hand. I was so shocked. We were all so shocked. We all looked around at each other. We didn't know where the old man had gotten it, because we were real poor. Two of my uncles had to borrow on their accounts at the trading store for the money I had in my purse. But there it was, a silver dollar so big and shiny in my grandfather's hand. Well, I was so shocked and everyone was so shocked that we all started crying right there at that junction of the Indian road and the paved highway. I wanted to be a little girl again, running after the old man when he hurried with his long legs to the corn fields or went for water down to the river. He was old then and his eyes were turned grey and he didn't do much anymore, just drive the wagon and chop a little bit of wood. But I just held him and I just held him so tightly.

Later on, I don't know what happened to the silver dollar. I guess it had a date of 1907 on it. But I kept it for a long time because I guess I wanted to have it when I remembered my home country. What I did in between then and now is another story. That's the time I moved away.*

There are a great many parallels between Pueblo experiences and the remarks that have been made about South Africa and the Caribbean countries—similarities in experiences so far as language is concerned. More specifically, with the experience of English being imposed upon the people. The Pueblo people, of course, have seen intruders come and intruders go. The first they watched come were the Spaniards; while the Spaniards were there, things had to be conducted in Spanish. But as the old stories say, if you wait long enough, they'll go. And sure enough, they went. Then another bunch came in. And old stories say, well, if you wait around long enough, not so much that they'll go, but at least their ways will go. One wonders now, when you see what's happening to technocratic-industrial culture, now that we've used up most of the sources of energy, you think perhaps the old people are right.

But anyhow, our experience with English has been different because the Bureau of Indian Affairs schools were so terrible that we never heard of Shakespeare. There was Dick and Jane, and I can remember reading that the robins were heading south for winter, but I knew that all winter the robins were around Laguna. It took me a long time to figure out what was going on. I worried for quite a while about the robins because they didn't leave in the winter, not realizing that the textbooks were written in Boston. The big textbook companies are up here in Boston and *their* robins do go south in the winter. But this freed us and encouraged us to stay with our narratives. Whatever literature we received at school (which was damn little), at home the storytelling, the special regard for telling and bringing together through the telling, was going on constantly. It has continued, and so we have a great body of classical oral literature, both in the narratives and in the chants and songs.

As the old people say, "If you can remember the stories, you will be all right. Just remember the stories." And, of course, usually when they say that to you, when you are young, you wonder what in the world they mean. But when I returned—I had been away from Laguna Pueblo for a couple of years, well more than a couple of years after college and so forth—I returned to Laguna and I went to Laguna-Acoma high school to visit an English class, and I was wondering how the telling was continuing, because Laguna Pueblo, as the anthropologists have said, is one of the more acculturated pueblos. So I walked into this high school English class and there they were sitting, these very beautiful Laguna and Acoma kids. But I knew that out in their lockers they had cassette tape recorders, and I knew that at home they had stereos, and they were listening to "Kiss" and Led Zeppelin and all those other things. I was almost afraid, but I had to ask—I had with me a book of short fiction (it's called *The Man to Send Rain Clouds* [New York: Viking Press, 1974]), and among the stories of other Native American writers, it has stories that I have written and Simon Ortiz has written. And there is one particular story in the book about the killing of a state policeman in New Mexico by three Acoma Pueblo men. It was an act that was committed in the early fifties. I was afraid to ask, but I had to. I looked at the class and I said, "How many of you heard this story before you read it in the book?" And I was prepared to hear this crushing truth that indeed the anthropologists were right about the old traditions dying out. But it was amazing, you know, almost all but one or two students raised their hands. They had heard that story, just as Simon and I had heard it, when we were young. That was my first indication that storytelling continues on. About half of them had heard it in English, about half of them had heard it in Laguna. I think again, getting back to one of the original statements, that if you begin to look at the core of the importance of the language and how it fits in with the culture, it is the *story* and the feeling of the story which matters more than what language it's told in.

One of the other advantages that we have enjoyed is that we have always been able to stay with the land. The stories cannot be separated from geographical locations, from actual physical places within the land. We were not relocated like so many Native American groups who were torn away from our ancestral land. And the stories are so much a part of these places that it is almost impossible for future generations to lose the stories because there are so many imposing geological elements. Just as Houston Baker was speaking about the mesas—there are such gigantic boulders—you cannot *live* in that land without asking or looking or noticing a boulder or rock. And there's always a story. There's always at least one story connected with those places. So this is again a kind of—if it's an advantage, or at least, I don't know whether it's fair to call it an advantage—it's just a fact.

I had one other thing to tell you about humor. One of the things about the attitude about language at home is that people are very suspicious of prepared speeches and preconceived words that someone has to say. And when old men come to pray—praying is also speaking to the people—and of course with the oral tradition, it is almost always a kind of extemporaneous act. And I think I am not one of the better practitioners of this act. But one of the other things I wanted to throw out to you was a little bit on the idea of humor. I mention this simply because a great many of the stories that are told contain within them simultaneously a wide range of emotional dimensions. So when you hear a story, a story that is supposed to be consoling somebody, it will often be a funny story although the occasion is sad. We have quite a number of funeral stories which are very funny. And this, of course, is not peculiar to Pueblo culture alone. One of the things that you will notice is that often in the stories there will be a movement toward a balance—the funny with the serious—and this goes back, this balance and this inclusion, the all-inclusive dynamic goes back to the Creation, and back to one of the basic Pueblo religious concepts. And what I have *for you* today is a short excerpt about humor. I mention that this is oftentimes something people from outside the Pueblo will not understand. They will think that something is funny, and it is comedy, and we put it over here; or something is serious and *must be* put over here [indicating].

If you go to Hopi for the summer dances, you will see the clowns, you will see the mud-head clowns carrying on in a most outrageous way and in a delightfully risqué manner. People who don't understand the place of humor in Pueblo culture will be very much taken aback by that. The same with the stories. Many times when I read a narrative like "Home Country," people won't laugh at the parts where you should laugh because they think that the story is basically a sad story. But the humor is always there, even with the most sacred or solemn. Just as serious reminders occur at joyous occasions. This is from an article by Emory Sekaquaptwea about Hopi clowning. It concerns the punning which the Hopi clowns are famous for:

> Because the Pueblo vision of language stems out of a world view which is inclusive rather than exclusive, the Hopi clowns do not hesitate to use English or any other language in order to get laughs with elaborate puns. This complex and slightly arcane Hopi pun illustrates one of the many directions that has been taken by traditional Pueblo people with the English language.

I'll tell you one I heard long ago. When it was time for this young clown man to make his confession, this is a part of the dance in which the clans are mocked or criticized in hopes of bettering them again, he jumped up and said, "*Ai, Ei,* geology, geology. *Ai, ei.*" Then he made a beautiful little breakdown of this word so that it has Hopi meaning.

"You probably think that I am talking about this *geology* which is a white man's study about something or other. Well, that's not it," he says. "What it really is, is that I have a grandmother, and, you know, she being poor and ugly, nobody would have anything to do with her. She is running around all summer long out in the fields, doing a man's job. It breaks her down. She would go out there every day with no shoes and so her feet were not very dainty, not very feminine. If you pick up her foot and look at the sole, it is all cracked, and that is what I am talking about when I say *geology*."

Every Hopi can put that together. *"Tsiya"* means "to crack" and *leetsi* means things "placed in a row." So these cracks are in a row on the bottom of the feet. *Geology. Tsiya-leetsi.* [Emory Sekaquaptewa, "One More Smile for a Hopi Clown," PARABOLA].

Thus, even in the most sacred of the ceremonies, traditional Hopis see no reason not to use an English word to get a laugh, a laugh being their sacred duty and a part of the whole overall ceremony. Delight in the power of language, and the effect achieved by juxtaposing language and world views is foremost in the Pueblo view. Dennis Brutus talked about the "yet unborn" as well as "those from the past," and how we are still *all* in *this* place, and language—the storytelling—is our entryway of passing or being with them, of being together again. When Aunt Suzie told her stories, she would tell a younger child to go open the door so that our esteemed predecessors may bring in their gifts to us. "They are out there," Aunt Suzie would say. "Let them come in. They're here, they're here with us *within* the stories."

I last visited her about four months ago. She is 106, and so if you walk into the room and try to ask her how many years she was at Carlisle Indian School—a direct question—she says she doesn't remember. But if you just let her speak her mind, every-thing that she says is very clear. And while I was there, she said, "Well, I'll be leaving here soon. I think I'll be leaving here next week, and I will be going over to the Cliff House." She said, "It's going to be real good to get back over there." I was listening, and I was thinking of her house at Paguate, at Paguate village, which is north of Laguna. And she continued on, "Well" (and she gave her Indian name) "my mother's sister will be there. She has been living there. She will be there and we will be over there, and I will get a chance to write down these stories I've been telling you." And it wasn't until she said it was her mother's sister who would be there that I realized she wasn't talking about dying or death at all. She was talking about "going over there," and she meant it as a journey, a journey that perhaps we can only begin to understand through an appreciation for the boundless capacity of language which, through storytelling, brings us together, despite great distances between cultures, despite great distances in time.

Leslie A. Fiedler

Literature as an Institution:
The View from 1980

We live at a time when literature, high and low, has ceased to be an independent, self-perpetuating institution; yet it is more institutionalized than ever. The notion of literature as an institution responsible only to itself (always more than myth than fact perhaps) has haunted the mind of the West ever since the Renaissance attempted to set song and story free from established religion. At first this meant little more than changing masters—becoming not independent, but dependent on the needs and demands of the court rather than the church. But with the invention of printing, the growth of literacy, and especially, the appearance of a "free market," literature seemed on the verge of total emancipation. To be sure, some writers found in the new economic context an occasion for a new kind of subservience to the marketplace. But the commodities such hucksters produced—as critics at that point began to insist—were subliterature, or paraliterature. "Real literature," though packaged and distributed side by side with commodity literature, was something quite different; it was responsive not to the laws of supply and demand, but to standards established by contemporary critics, the visible legislators of the invisible "Republic of Letters."

In the last decades of the twentieth century, however, they themselves have been co-opted by the university as completely as the hucksters were by the marketplace. Though some of us continue to speak of "Great Books," as if humanism were still a living movement instead of one more classroom subject, we all know in our hearts that literature is effectively what we teach in departments of English; or conversely, what we teach in departments of English is literature. Within that closed definitional circle, we perform the rituals by which we cast out unworthy pretenders from our ranks and induct true initiates, guardians of the standards by which all song and story ought presumably to be judged.

The penetration of academia by critics, as opposed to scholars and literary historians, along with the living poets and novelists about whom the critics wrote, did not occur until a generation or two ago. Robert Frost was, I believe, the first official writer-in-residence at any American college; he arrived at the University of Michigan in 1927, only a few years after his verse had been accepted into the English curriculum. Yet even after colleges in the United States had begun to teach contemporary works in the mother tongue, the prevailing academic definition of literature was still very different from that which moved most leading writers of the time.

The former definition was sustained by succeeding generations of old-style professors, the sons, or less often the daughters, of the original American ruling class, who were sometimes eccentric but always genteel. Typically they had been trained in German universities, whence they returned, convinced of the virtues of rigorous Teutonic *Philologie*. But their tastes were determined by the values of Victorian England, which, to be sure, they believed to be universal and immortal, though they were being challenged even then by the extra-academic exponents of a rival definition of literature. However, those self-styled avant-gardists and experimentalists seemed to their opponents to be juvenile and perverse, and their francophile assault on the Anglo Saxon/Germanic canon seemed to be more a bad joke than a real threat.

Nevertheless, in the years just before and after World War I, the taste of the disreputable dissenters triumphed in the larger literary world, and it seemed only a matter of time before their taste would carry the day inside the university. Its spokesmen had redeemed the reputations of Herman Melville and Walt Whitman and upped the value of the hitherto depressed literary stock of John Donne and Gerard Manley Hopkins, while they downgraded the value of Milton and Shelley, Longfellow and Tennyson. Moreover, though most of the earliest New Critics came from the same privileged caste as their academic opposites, they sought to de-bourgeoisfy themselves, to pass into the non-class or meta-class of Bohemians or Intellectuals.

In any case, they were, by and large, not academics; their occasional brief flirtations with the classroom ended in such comic dénouements as Ezra Pound's expulsion from the faculty of Wabash College after he had harbored strippers in his room. They prided themselves on being amateurs and dilettantes; or if they were professionals at all, they were journalists, book reviewers, and especially contributors to, founders and editors of "little magazines"—adversary literary quarterlies. Often transient, occasionally longer-lasting, these journals ranged from those that were catholic in their approach and appeal, such as *Hound and Horn,* to those that took their stand on the political Right, like *Criterion* (whose editorial columns found fascism more acceptable than communism), the *Southern Review* (subsidized by Huey Long), the *Kenyon Review* (in some ways its successor), and *Furioso* (one of whose original editors was a particularly notorious CIA agent). Others paid allegiance to the Left, like *New Masses* (whose staff consisted largely of orthodox Stalinists) and the *Partisan Review* (which began with the Trotskyist split-off from Stalinism).

What they all had in common, which made it possible for some contributors to pass back and forth between, for example, the *Kenyon Review* and the *Partisan Review,* was a commitment to modernism and a hatred for the bourgeois middle: middle-class morality, middling politics, and middlebrow taste. Not even on the extreme Left did the extra-academics object to the elitism of the old academy. Instead they accused the professorial establishment of inadequate elitism: a failure to spot certain kinds of pretentious or pious *kitsch,* and a complementary blindness to the merits of experimental, highbrow literature.

This situation prevailed well into the 1950s, well past my own entry into college teaching. I can remember, for instance, those tedious speeches delivered year after year by the current presidents of the Modern Language Association (MLA) deploring the incursion of "modernists" into university departments of English. And I can recall finding myself homeless in 1953 in Bloomington, Indiana, where I had gone to teach a summer course. The house I thought I had rented was snatched away from me at the very last moment by its landlord, a local "scholar," who had learned that I was "one of them," i.e., a critic. What made it even worse is that I had been invited, not as a member of the English Department proper, but as a visiting lecturer in the School of Letters—that oddly hybrid Trojan horse, out of Philip Rahv by John Crowe Ransom. Indeed, like me, other critics had by then begun to swarm out of the bellies of similar treacherous machines into beleaguered academia. And what a motley crew we were: not only were we bearers of subversive aesthetic doctrines, but a good many of us at least were also the offspring of ethnically inferior, non-English-speaking stock; our veneer of Anglo-Saxon polite culture was no more than a generation thick.

It was, however, a rear-guard action that the old-style defenders of the citadel were fighting. By the end of the 1950s, the former outsiders were insiders, although they were allowed in at first, perhaps, for reasons more demographic than ideological. The end of World War II had seen the influx into colleges and universities of vast hordes of government-subsidized students. Many of them were the first members of their families ever to be exposed to higher education. And to teach the succeeding waves of the continuing invasion, new faculty had to be recruited from the first waves. These were the sons and daughters, though still mainly sons, of working-class or petty-bourgeois parents (who were not even predominantly Northern European, much less *echt* Anglo-Saxon; and who, after a while, were overwhelmingly Eastern European and Jewish) and graduates of

land grant universities or city colleges, such cultural arrivistes
more often began their literary careers by reading or contribu-
ting to the *Partisan Review* and the *Kenyon Review* rather than
by submitting articles to the *PMLA*. Their elitism was, therefore, quite different from that of their predecessors. But once
they were ensconced in departments of English, they proved to
be equally narrow and exclusive.

To their WASP predecessors, who were born of upper-class
parents, educated at quality schools, and sustained by inherited
wealth or marriage to money, an academic career represented
merely a marginally acceptable vocation. But to the "new pro-
fessorate," it represented a way of making it into a position of
unaccustomed prestige, if not of power; it was a strategy for
social climbing without seeming to "sell out" to the world of
hucksterism or venal politics. I am not suggesting that they
(*we,* I suppose I should say) did this deliberately; but it was
at least subintended, and, in any case, it worked! It worked so
well, in fact, that after a while those who were initially regarded
as interlopers began to seem more at home than anyone else.

Indeed, by the late seventies, the few remaining antiacademic
critics tended to be primarily WASPs—either piously moralistic
defenders of the "eternal verities" like John Gardner, or snide
exponents of high camp, like Gore Vidal. However self-serving
the case made by these two novelists against the academization
of American fiction is, they are responding to a genuine problem. Not only are most of the novels prized by academic critics
the work of writers who have sought shelter in the university,
but their chief readership consists of teachers and students who
study them in the classroom.

Almost no novels, in fact, seem any longer to be ends in
themselves. As words on the page, they represent transitional
stages on the way to a final form: if they are adjudged "high
literature," they are represented by a diagram on the black-
board; or if classified as "low literature," they become images
on the screen. English majors are taught to deplore the latter

transformation as vulgarization, although it is, perhaps, better understood as the democratization of art, which is desirable as well as inevitable in a mass society. This seems especially true in the case of the novel, which was from the start a salable commodity: the product not of lonely genius and tradition, but of technology and the marketplace.

What seems to me to be aberrant and unnatural is the nineteenth century attempt to separate from the ordinary run of fiction the "art novel"; by which I mean certain dense, complex works that are immediately available to only a tiny minority of readers, and later—with a teacher's help—to a slightly larger minority. As a result of this misguided taxonomic venture, teachers of English have indoctrinated their students to regard all prose fiction as necessarily divided into the majority novel and the minority novel, and only the latter is considered to be worth teaching or learning.

In recent days, to be sure, as enrollment in traditional English courses shrinks, even traditionally trained professors feel compelled to offer courses in what they condescendingly call "popular literature," and think of as yet another "special area" of literary study. But majority literature is essentially nonspecialized, because it is all that remains of what was literature, whole and undivided, before the institution of universities. Courses that include nothing but what their instructors consider not quite "real literature" end up by seeming more ghettoized than specialized. Moreover, because they employ modes of analysis invented for high literature, they turn both of those modes as well as the works to which they are applied into unwitting parodies.

In the realm of poetry, a similar division has been made between two kinds of verse: one is typically set to music and therefore customarily not read but heard by a mass audience, most of whose members think they hate poetry. The others are printed, and read as part of a classroom assignment or, if they are listened to at all, are listened to at poetry readings, which are typically organized under academic auspices in after-hour classrooms. The audience that gathers on such occasions is likely to consist largely of students, many of whom are present because they have been ordered to attend by their teachers. In the fifties, such readings were usually held in the seedy bohemias that surrounded college campuses; when they moved on to the campus in the late sixties, they took place in field houses, gymnasiums, in the midst of smoke-ins or at demonstrations against the war in Vietnam. But such occasions have also been assimilated to the institution that sponsors them, so that at present even the returning laureates of the defunct cultural revolution, an aging Gary Synder or an Allen Ginsburg, for example, are presumed to have met standards from which only popular song verse is exempted.

In terms of such "standards," all printed song and story is classified as "junk" or "mere entertainment," (i.e., *non*-literature), if they opt for sentimentality rather than irony, the literal rather than the symbolic, or the commonplace rather than the recherché. On the level of style and structure, prose narrative must reject not only the conventional happy ending and the Maupassant-O. Henry hook but also all undue emphasis on plot and character. Similarly, poetry must eschew end rhyme, regular metre, and stanzaic form. In the end, the institutionalized elite taste of the late twentieth century regards as substandard almost everything that naive and uninstructed readers are likely to recognize as a story or poem.

But this means, in effect, the exclusion of anything which the children of such readers can comprehend, even after they enter college, without the aid of a qualified teacher. It should be clear, therefore, that whatever the origins of the definition of literature that determine the curriculum of classes in "Eng Lit," one of its functions is to guarantee opportunities for the display of exegetical skills to Ph.D.s in literature. It is not entirely a one-way transaction, however, because what provides ego-satisfaction to certain professors also affords a chosen minority of students—hard-core English majors and fellow travellers—the sense of being initiated into a self-made, self-perpetuating aristocracy of taste. For such teachers and students, literature is totally identified with the texts—the words on the page they scrutinize together. Consequently, they have little difficulty in believing either that "the medium is the message," or that print is the ultimate medium toward which all preceding mediums represent a slow ascent, and from which all succeeding mediums represent a regrettable decline.

Therefore, any work that calls into question this article of faith by proving to be translatable into post-Gutenburg forms without loss, or even worse, with some gain of affect and authenticity, challenge the very *raison d'être* of professional teachers of English. This is why they find themselves at the moment defending high culture against the media, which simply means all the ways of transmitting song and story that are more generally accessible than print.

But this was not the enemy against whom we were contending when we made our entry into university departments of English. It was against our genteel predecessors and their obsolete notions of what constituted literary excellence that we sought to defend the modernist works we loved and a definition of literature that justified our taste. Though we are still defending that definition, qualified a little to allow for certain post-modernist developments, we find ourselves battling not our old academic opponents, but the mass audience, which reads best sellers and science fiction or, more often, simply watches sitcoms, cop shows, and soap operas on television— as a good many of us do.

I read the other day of a totally unreconstructed highbrow who boasted that she had never even opened a best seller and knew no one who had. But that is not a boast I can make; and I suspect that a large number of my academic colleagues, plus most of my students—sometimes openly, sometimes behind closed curtains—break their strict diet of required *belles-lettres* in order to satisfy their hunger for the irresponsible fantasy, shameful concupiscence, and shameful tears and laughter that are released by popular fiction. Yet we do not ordinarily face up to our hypocrisy in this regard; much less do we understand how we have been persuaded to accept a definition of literature that we are driven helplessly to betray.

Universal schooling, I think, lies at the root of it all. Originally fought for as a right, it has long since become an obligation; subsidized by the state because it not only trains students in the vocational skills necessary to the economic well-being of us all, but also inculcates values that sustain our economy. In the immigrant society of the United States, this has involved the homogenization of diverse peoples, many of them raised in pre-industrial cultures where the Protestant work ethic was never invented. Of all courses in the standard school curriculum, English is the one most easily co-opted (and for that reason, perhaps, it remains the most widely required) into the service of the melting pot ideal: the instant WASPification and bourgeoisification of all Americans, whatever their class or ethnic origin.

In the primers of the early twentieth century, the children of the foreign-born were taught, along with reading and writing, to change their underwear frequently and sleep with the windows open, to honor their mothers and fathers, respect the police, work hard, and save their money. And their children and children's children are presented still with similar norms embodied in those insufferably pink and white, well-adjusted little WASPlets called Dick and Jane. At least they were still so-called when my own sons and daughters were in the first and second grades; I have no doubt that though the names may have been changed, just such spotless, smiling kids, plus their dog, cat, and eternally adolescent parents ("O see father run! Funny funny father!") continue to stir envy and encourage emulation in children like me, who had neither dog nor cat, only Yiddish speaking grandparents and a father who never joined me at playing baseball.

Such behavior modification is continued in English classes

(not maliciously, but in all good will) up through grade eight and on into high school, where for many years—at the suggestion of certain old-line Anglophile professors—American teenagers were required to slog their way through Scott's genteelly anti-semitic Tory romance, *Ivanhoe,* and George Eliot's insufferably moral Victorian fable, *Silas Marner.* Nor does this process cease in English grade thirteen, which, though still often required, seems somehow not quite so oppressive in a college setting, where at least guards do not prowl the halls, exit doors are not locked to prevent truancy, and it has been given the new names "Freshman Composition" or "Rhetoric I." For a while in the late sixties, such courses were on many campuses abolished, made optional, or turned into opportunities for free expression, self-examination and amateur therapy. But ten years later, the cry of "Back to Basics" went up, and in response, research papers returned to replace the journal jottings and group gropes of the sixties. So, even though certain superficial changes in manners have persisted (freshman teachers continue still to sleep with their freshman students, and both continue to smoke pot) in all essential respects the *status quo ante-bellum* has been restored.

Thus freshman comp has once more been openly revealed as being what it never ceased covertly to be: a last desperate attempt to impose on our multilingual, multidialectal population a single correct Anglo-American dialect, brainwashing us out of our various mother tongues—the demotic linguistic codes of home, street, and schoolyard. At the same time it teaches us to be ashamed of the demotic literary culture that we acquire outside the classroom. That culture includes not only pre- or extra-Gutenburg material like ball-bouncing songs, traditional prayers, riddles, limericks, jokes, parodies, and the jingles written on toilet walls; but stuff transmitted by post-Gutenburg media: popular songs, advertising slogans, the monster lore of genre movies, and the adventures—comic, heroic, or erotic—of characters on television shows. And it extends finally even to the less reputable products of the Gutenburg process itself: comic books, greeting card verse, the poetry used as filler in newspapers, pulp stories, sentimental novels, and so on.

In freshman courses in composition, the grounds for that rejection can theoretically be made clear, as, presumably, they have never been. Most teachers of the various levels of high-school English are incapable of distinguishing sharply between high and low literature. Here or nowhere, beginning teachers of composition tend to think; therefore, now or never we must teach these majors in nursing, engineering, or business administration that even the most distinguished laureates of popular culture provide pleasures that are different not only in kind from the delights of high literature, but that differ in effect as well: drugging rather than stimulating the mind, enslaving rather than liberating the spirit. And when their students resist what seems to those teachers so apparent, they are likely to blame not the doctrine they espouse, but the philistine society that rejects it.

I myself first taught comp as a teaching assistant some forty years ago, and for fifteen or twenty years, such courses constituted a major part of my load. Yet I can remember dreaming all that time that someday I would get to teach real courses in real literature, as rigorous and difficult as those I had grimly endured—and only in retrospect relished—on my way to a Ph.D. I suspect that even now young teachers who are required to teach required comp keep telling themselves, as I did, that once they preside over upperclassmen and graduate students, they will no longer have to play the degrading role of thought police enforcing "standards"; but will be able instead, like kindly commissars, "patiently to explain," and thus to convince mature men and women to accept freely the notion that political democracy does not entail cultural leveling. That dream is not altogether delusory. After a while, we preach to the converted; i.e., those who are convinced, like us, that all literature is divided into what panders to the ignorant many, and what appeals to the learned few, and that only the latter should be taught in class or preserved in libraries. Yet the overburdened taxpayers and generous alumni who make possible those classes and sustain those libraries have utterly different assumptions about the nature of literature. They demonstrate this by buying in large numbers books of which we disapprove and making smash hits of television sitcoms that we despise. Why then do they continue to subsidize not just the critical establishment but those works that it calls high art? Is it sheer hypocrisy—the tribute vice pays to virtue? Or does it reflect a need on the part of the majority to believe that what they read by preference is in some sense taboo?

To be sure, occasionally legislators, school boards, and organizations of parents attempt to impose a tyranny of the majority on us all by striking from required reading lists, removing from library shelves, and even on occasion burning books that challenge reigning values. Customarily, however, they advocate censorship after-the-fact not on aesthetic grounds, but on moral or ideological ones—invoking the shibboleths of patriotism, decency, and chastity, or suggesting that certain works encourage violence or reinforce obnoxious ethnic and sexist stereotypes. Since the works they typically condemn include not only those that elitist critics consider trash—*Starsky and Hutch,* for instance, or hard pornography—but some that they prize as high art, like *Justine, Tropic of Cancer,* and *Lady Chatterley's Lover,* such critics feel impelled to resist the bourgeois book burners on all fronts, untroubled by the fact that in their classrooms they seek to impose an equal and opposite tyranny of the minority—not, to be sure, by police power or vigilante action, but only by giving low grades or withholding degrees.

There is, indeed, a sense in which the latter tyranny is a by-product of the former, since the notion of high culture received its final formulation in the multipurpose American university, which is itself one of the chief institutions of American mass

culture. Paradoxically, however, the hierarchal view of literature at its heart is a vestige of a defunct, class-structured society, no longer viable in the world of mass communications and
advanced technology, whether capitalist or socialist. Yet the
traditional Left has always shared the hierarchal assumptions
about literature of the genteel Victorians and their modernist
Western critics. Karl Marx himself set the example by devoting
much of his first book, *The Holy Family*, to an attack on the
idol of mid-nineteenth century working-class readers, Eugene
Sue. It was partly Sue's shameless sensationalism that offended
Marx, but even more it was the marketplace success of Sue's
The Wandering Jew and *The Mysteries of Paris.*

Such success, Marx felt, could only be explained on the
grounds of the manipulation of popular taste by moneyed interests, the masters of the media. And this conspiracy theory
has continued to haunt left wing German academics ever since,
perhaps most especially Herbert Marcuse and the members of
the Frankfurt School. Nor are American antiacademic Marxists
immune; so that even that anti-textbook of our own dissenting
sixties, *The Politics of Literature,* though it bravely attacked
the by then long-dead New Criticism, made no defense of
the post-Gutenburg culture preferred by the majority audience. Moreover, many of the essays included were so ostenta-
tiously scholarly that they seemed, finally, as much aimed at
ensuring tenure and promotion for the authors as at subverting
the institutionalized teachings of English.

Nor is it possible to attribute the elitism of such self-declared
dissidents to what is least American in their thought. The native
populist tradition that also influences them is by no means immune to a yearning toward high literature and a contempt for
mass culture. Even V. L. Parrington, most eloquent spokesman
for that point of view, considered James Branch Cabell's pretentious, essentially shallow pornographic fantasy, *Jurgen,* to be
real art in a sense that Harriet Beecher Stowe's *Uncle Tom's
Cabin,* despite its sympathetic politics, was not. But she is the

test case for us all. Invisible to the newest neoclassicists like
Derrida and Lacan, she was equally invisible to D. H. Lawrence
and F. O. Matthiessen, who established the canon of American
classics we feel able to teach without surrendering our hierarchal view of literature.

To confess now that the uneducated taste that has made
Stowe the longest-lasting of all best sellers is superior to the
taste of the critical establishment would be to question our
own authority as teachers. Not only reactionaries, conserva-
tives, and liberals remain authoritarian in this sense; but (even
more so, perhaps) revolutionaries, including the recent self-
appointed tribunes of blacks and women are authoritarian. It
is understandable enough that James Baldwin, as an Afro-
American and a male, has always found what he calls "Everybody's Protest Novel" to be despicable art and contemptible
politics. But I was a little appalled to discover that Ann Douglas's recent *The Feminization of American Culture* treats the
only major work of fiction produced by a woman in the mid-
nineteenth century as a seductive piece of trash—a first step
toward the ultimate degradation of our literature.

Mrs. Stowe has had her defenders, to be sure. Ralph Waldo
Emerson, for instance, remarked (with only the slightest note
of condescension) that her novel was read "with equal pleasure
in the parlor, the kitchen and the nursery." And Leo Tolstoy
concurred, finding her book one of the few which joined together, rather than further divided, already sundered elements
of the population. But since the works of both Emerson and
Tolstoy (including *Anna Karenina* which Tolstoy disavowed in
the name of his own principles) have been accepted into the
canon of high literature, their views are now studied in the
context of the tradition that they tried to subvert. Neither
Emerson nor Tolstoy, in any case, was ever in a position to influence university teaching. But Madame Mao, who shared their
enthusiasm for Mrs. Stowe, was. Indeed, she was even further
along in her capitulation to the feminized mass culture of

America by suggesting that—as a part of the reform of higher learning and in the name of the Cultural Revolution—the study of the classics both Eastern and Western, be replaced by the reading of two American best sellers that were descended from Mrs. Stowe: Louisa May Alcott's *Little Women,* and Margaret Mitchell's *Gone With the Wind.*

The cultural revolution in our own country has had no such distinguished elder spokeswoman. Feminized mass culture has been abandoned, without a struggle, to the book stalls in supermarkets displaying women's romances which, as sexual mores change, grow even more pornographic, without ever ceasing to be sentimental. They have lost especially to daytime television, where the soap operas create similar erotic and domestic dreams for the largest audience of all. That revolution did, however, find spokes*men*: male, white, middle-class discontents, most of whom were academics; just as the constituency they addressed were students—campus activists.

To the latter, the reform of the university, which provided them a home away from home and a refuge from the draft, meant primarily its deliverance from the control of "the military-industrial complex." They were not, in any case, especially interested in novels (rock music was their favorite art form and genre movies ran a close second); and insofar as fiction concerned them all, they pressed for including in the English curriculum certain twentieth century "youth best sellers," ranging from Jack Kerouac's *On the Road* and Ken Kesey's *One Flew Over the Cuckoo's Nest* to Robert Heinlein's *Stranger in a Strange Land* and J. R. R. Tolkien's ring trilogy.

Oddly enough, the elder statesmen whom they made their cultural gurus cared no more for these books than they did for the music or films preferred by the young. Some were basically indifferent to all art, like that afficionado of technology, Buckminster Fuller. Others were elitists of the old school, like Marshall McLuhan, who began as an acolyte of the New Critics, and whose favorite authors remained always Gerard Manley

Hopkins and James Joyce; or Norman O. Brown, an unreconstructed classicist whose sensibility had been fixed forever (never mind his later discovery of Freud, Marx and Jonathan Swift) by Hesiod and Ovid; or Herbert Marcuse, a left-wing academic, who to the end of his days quarrelled with the pop taste that had made the right-wing militarist Robert Heinlein laureate-in-chief of the sixties.

Yet even before those young activists turned into middle-aged faculty members in the late seventies, novels like *Stranger in a Strange Land* had begun to infiltrate the curriculum. This opening up was partly a matter of cold-blooded hucksterism: a way of attracting additional "full-time equivalents" in a time of declining enrollments. But it also suited the needs of certain aging professors who had grown as weary of their areas of specialization as of the students themselves. They were joined by some of their junior colleagues, who were not too much older than the undergraduate apostles of the Counter Culture, and impelled therefore in a kind of sibling rivalry to claim such underground favorites as their own. After all, they reminded their students, it was they who had fought the good fight against their academic predecessors for yesterday's youth cult books: Proust and Mann and Joyce, Fitzgerald and Hemingway and Faulkner, Nathanael West and Henry Roth; nor were they about to surrender their place at the head of the avant-garde.

As the job situation grew ever grimmer, however, it seemed to the younger faculty less important to please a constituency that changed every four years than to win the esteem of their tenured older peers. To do so they had to play the institutional game by its own rules: begin by publishing in reputable journals rigorous essays on canonical books, then produce a major book formidable enough to be issued under the aegis of a distinguished university press.

Consequently, those junior professors who have not completely abandoned the contemporary have shifted their attention from novelists like Robert Heinlein and Robert Pirsig and

Richard Adams, who provide the largest young audiences with immediate pleasure, to others who afford much smaller groups the mediated satisfaction of classroom exegesis. Some of the latter, John Barth, for instance, and William Gass, have made their permanent homes in the university; but even those who visit the academy only from time to time, like Vladimir Nabokov and Donald Barthelme, or those who spurn it utterly, like Thomas Pynchon, seem, like the former, to write as if for such exegesis. All of them, therefore, gifted though they may be, end up by addressing merely themselves and their postmodernist critics, who, in turn, address only each other.

"Autotelic" is what their modernist forebears—the New Critics—labelled such criticism. But they were acutely aware, at least, that the craft they practised has not always been so self-referential. When first reinvented in the West by the self-styled humanists, it had (Sir Philip Sidney's *Defense of Poetry* is the classic example in English) addressed itself to living writers, to whom it gave, before the fact, formulas for literary excellence, and, after the fact, good or bad marks. The prescriptive/proscriptive function of criticism has, however, been largely surrendered these days to classes in freshman composition; while the evaluative function survives on all levels of college instruction in English, as well as in newspaper bookreviewing. But neither function is any longer performed by serious criticism.

Now the mediational or apologetic function was central to the audience-oriented school that next rose to preeminence. Such early examples of the approach as the Marquis de Sade's *Idées sur le roman* and Wordsworth's *Preface to the Lyrical Ballads* responded to the growing split in the emerging mass audience, which tended to divide along class lines as literacy spread to groups not yet inducted into the traditional culture, and along generational lines, as radically new styles in prose and verse succeeded each other with confusing rapidity. Until the first decades of this century, most major critics were still desperately trying to put Humpty Dumpty together again by explaining to a philistine public what was obscure or unfamiliar in contemporary art, or by defending what seemed deliberately offensive. But in the end their efforts proved futile. Larger and larger numbers of readers continued not merely to reject novels and poems highly prized by such critics, but to ignore them as well, until, like the authors of those neglected works, the critics began to consider their exclusion a testimonial to their worth.

Nonetheless, the New Critics and their present day heirs did not at first completely abandon the missionary goals of their predecessors. Instead they narrowed them down, addressing only these alienated sons and daughters of the philistines who sat at their feet in classes of English. And in the process, the New Criticism became the New Pedagogy, eventuating in such quasi-scriptural textbooks as Brooks and Warren's *Understanding Poetry*. But as modernism yielded to postmodernism, and as even newer formalisms emerged, the audience came to seem as irrelevant to serious critics as that of the author. All that mattered was the text—or rather, as the fashionable phrase has it—the subtext. Despite all of that, academic criticism is no longer truly autotelic, since the critic-pedagogues who produce it are paid for doing so by a society that considers them part of the professional cadre that turns raw English majors into the next generation of fully credentialled critic-pedagogues, capable of training a third generation and so on.

Moreover, the extracurricular essays and books, which the new formalists theoretically publish for exclusive consumption by their peers, are entered into their dossiers and scrutinized by departmental promotion committees, provosts, and deans. But this means that for a long time the academic critic writes, or at least publishes, out of economic necessity rather than free choice: first in order to avoid termination, then to rise in academic rank. Even after he has reached the final level of his vertical ascent, continuing publication makes possible for him lateral movement to more prestigious schools, more salubrious climes. Any challenge to the literary *status quo,* therefore, threatens not just individual teachers, but departments of English as a whole; indeed, the very departmental structure of the university, as well as the assumptions about professionalism, specialization and scholarship which underlie it are threatened.

Why then has the English Institute, which constitutes, as it were, the elite guard of such departments, sponsored this forum; and why it it now subsidizing the publication of essays like this one, which attacks values and standards in which most of its members believe? Can it be because they believe in tolerance more? Or are they, on the off chance that one or more of us dissenters may be right, cannily hedging their bets? Or do they suffer us gladly, knowing that at this point, all dissent, whether populist, feminist, Marxist, or Third World, can be assimilated, neutralized, sterilized, by paying those who teach it, and giving academic credit to students who take classes in it.

I find it disheartening, though also a little amusing, to grant that this may well be true. I have long been aware that just as the American supermarket can accommodate gourmet delicacies or health foods without losing its homogeneous character, or as commercial American television can find room for "Opera Live from the Met" without abandoning its leveling mission—so can the American university, without betraying its heritage, include both courses in elite literature and courses which attack the very concept by insisting that all song and story are now and have always been essentially one. If this is not the ultimate irony implicit in the situation which I have been examining, it is the last of which I am aware, the place, therefore, where (for now at least) I must end.

H. Bruce Franklin

English as an Institution: The Role of Class

When Leslie Fiedler asked me to make a presentation to the English Institute on "class biases" in "a forum dealing with certain biases and limitations built into the very structure of literature departments, and perhaps into the very definition of literature itself, as assumed by such departments," I felt as though I had just been invited to lecture to the American Medical Association on their prejudices against socialized medicine, or the American Correctional Officers Association on their biases in favor of prisons. After all, we professors of literature enjoy a relatively comfortable, privileged, and respected existence, which depends on society's agreeing with our own claim to valuable knowledge, profound intellection, social usefulness, and, above all, superior taste. So our very membership in the ranks of the professional class could possibly be jeopardized by our daring to examine the fundamental assumptions that legitimize our profession. Suppose the tax-paying public suddenly were to think of our scholarly books and articles, our canon of the great literary tradition, and even our doctorates as just a nice big suit of new clothes for the emperor? Well, I'm afraid this is not such a remote possibility, for that is exactly how most of the tax-paying public already regards our claims. If you don't think so, take another look at the *Modern Language Association Job List* or next year's budget for your own department.

Meanwhile, as we all know, literature departments around the country are being torn by tooth-and-claw struggles between the populist heretics and the canonical authorities. So discussions about class biases in literature departments are apt to be somewhat less calm than discussions of Stephen Crane's use of color imagery. Even less calm are the responses arising from the broader historical context in which this forum emerges.

This forum, like so many other things in our society today, represents one of the unresolved questions defined for us by the 1960s, and therefore many people in this room probably bring to our subject certain responses formed in and by the 1960s. Remember that it was at the very end of 1968 that our entire profession was rudely forced to confront the subject of our forum.

The year 1968 had begun with a devastating month-long humiliation of the American military behemoth throughout the southern half of Vietnam, a campaign described by our military and political leaders as "the last gasp" of the Vietnamese "enemy." A few weeks later, Martin Luther King, Jr., was assassinated, and simultaneous rebellions erupted in 125 cities in the United States. Within two months, dozens of American campuses became the scene of militant confrontations over CIA recruiters, chemical and biological warfare research, ROTC, and other direct involvement of the universities in the Indochina War. In June, Robert Kennedy, who had apparently just wrapped up the Democratic presidential nomination, was assassinated. In August, the Republican convention in Miami Beach had to be protected by armored troop carriers and tanks from a Black rebellion that spread from northwest Miami, bringing gunfights to within one mile of the convention headquarters. Later that month, tens of thousands of antiwar protesters battled the police, the national guard, and regular army units outside the Democratic convention in Chicago. Dozens of Black troops were arrested for refusing to participate in suppressing the demonstrators. Meanwhile, widespread rebellions broke out among the American soldiers and sailors in Vietnam. And the economy was already showing ominous signs of having been exhausted by the deficit financing of the Indochina War.

In December of 1968, at the Modern Language Association Convention in New York, the progenitors of our forum were beginning to take shape as a major panel entitled "The American

Scholar and the Crisis of Our Culture" and as a seminar, put together by a hodgepodge of faculty and graduate student political activists, entitled "Student Rebellions and the Teaching of
Literature." Then the physical confrontations of 1968 intruded
directly into the convention, as Louis Kampf, Chairman of the
Department of Literature at M.I.T., and two others were arrested for allegedly taping up a poster in the Americana hotel.
By the time four days of tumult were over, there had been a
sit-in, many mass meetings, much agitation and more consterna-
tion, while the Modern Language Association had taken a position condemning the Vietnam War, established the Commission
on the Status of Women, elected Louis Kampf into the succes-
sion to the presidency, and begun to become aware that the
question of class biases in literature departments could no longer
be buried under the floor along with Poe's tell-tale heart. The
reactions to what had taken place at the convention were
frenzied, and by the end of the 1969 spring term the trenches
had been dug right through our subject.

Out of that 1968 convention and the ensuing debates emerged
a seminal collection of essays, many of which were written by
participants in the fracas; titled *The Politics of Literature: Dissenting Essays on the Teaching of Literature,* this book is a pre-
requisite for serious discussion of our subject. *The Politics of
Literature* unified the activism of the 1960s with the ideological
reexamination forced by that activism, and summed up the
passionate, iconoclastic, and combative intellectual synthesis
that was emerging to challenge the accepted dogma of our profession. Looking backward, I think we can see that this volume
articulated the theoretical bases for a redefinition of literature
and a reshaping of the structure for the teaching of literature.
Thus it has also served as a prolegomenon for the work of re-
defining and reshaping that has gone on ever since.

The main achievement of these essays, most of which were
written in 1969 and 1970, was to define very clearly and to begin to explore the class biases, sexual biases, and ethnic biases in

the structure of literature departments as well as in their operational definition, evaluation, and presentation of literature. Several essays expose the feudal and bourgeois content of the literary tradition to which we are supposed to be loyal and toward which we are supposed to bend and push our students. For example, Sheila Delany's "Up Against the Great Tradition" gives a detailed picture of how most teachers of literature, partly through that literature, have "absorbed the myths of bourgeois society and are daily engaged in perpetuating them"[1] Following a path laid out by Raymond Williams in *The Long Revolution,* Delany incidentally demonstrates how "our vocabulary of praise and blame is full of words which dissolve class distinctions into moral categories. 'Gentle,' 'noble,' 'churl,' and 'villain' all originally designated social class, and only gradually came to represent the stereotyped moral character which the ruling class associated with various strata."[2] Barbara Kessel's brilliant essay, "Free, Classless, and Urbane," describes how her indoctrination into bourgeois ideology, taken to its most sophisticated level in her graduate-school training, was transformed into its opposite as she began to pay serious attention to what her working-class students had to say about the literature she was teaching. Kessel's essay is a stunning achievement, for within it she embodies a new methodological approach to literature, where the opposing perceptions of readers from different social classes interplay with the class contradictions within the work itself. Looking back on my own essay, "The Teaching of Literature in the Highest Academies of the Empire," probably the most polemical in this book of polemics, I realize that my work of the past ten years or so has largely been an attempt to develop and apply the principles baldly stated there. I argued that the canonization of a handful of literary works as "timeless," "universal," and transcendently "great" accomplished three interrelated purposes, all part of the appointed cultural mission of our literature departments:

1. This is a means of propagandizing the world view of these

works, which tend to be almost entirely the world view of white males from relatively privileged social classes in societies actively engaged in conquering and ruling other peoples.

2. Since the world view within this literature tends to reflect the world view of the social class choosing these canonical works, it reinforces both the authority and the position—ethical, social, and economic—of the professors of literature.

3. Above all, it substitutes a tiny part for the whole, demeaning as subliterary or otherwise unworthy of serious attention almost the entire body of the world's literature, especially popular literature (including science fiction, detective stories, westerns, and tales of adventure and romance), folk literature, oral literature, literature based on the experience of work, especially industrial work and domestic work, and almost all literature by nonwhite peoples.

Other essays in *The Politics of Literature* now seem like early formulations of work that was to mature later in the 1970s, especially in three areas. Wayne O'Neill's "The Politics of Bidialecticism" and William Labov's "The Logic of Nonstandard English" are well-developed models of explorations into the class assumptions of the language and usage we enforce in our special role as the verbal police force, committed to the law and order of prescriptive grammar. Martha Vicinus's essay on "The Study of Nineteenth-Century British Working-Class Poetry" foreshadows her own splendid investigations and those of many others into the proletarian literature that had been swept under the academic carpet. Richard Ohmann's essay, "Teaching and Studying Literature at the End of Ideology," was later included in his monumental study, one that every member of our profession should be required to read, *English in America: A Radical View of the Profession.* In this 1976 study, Ohmann asks and answers the questions most fundamental to the subject of this forum: How and why did English departments appear? What were they supposed to do then? What are they supposed to do now? How do they go about doing it? And what are the unexamined assumptions fundamental to both their structure and daily operations?

Let me attempt to sketch, as briefly as possible, a few especially relevant events in the history of English departments, drawing partly on work already published by Ohmann, myself, and others.

The first men bearing the title "Professor of English literature" appeared in America right on the eve of the Civil War, the struggle that began with the government of the United States in the hands of a rural, semi-feudal class of slave owners, together with their allies, and that ended with the hegemony of industrial capitalism. At first, the business of English professors was simply to "cultivate" young collegiate men of the privileged classes by training them, through the study of rhetoric and literature, to speak and write in a "cultured" style. This mission, which we would now call a service function, developed in the 1880s and 1890s into a specialized "study" of literature conceived of as a "professional activity" with its own independent claims to providing a benefit for the individual and for society.[3] The earlier service function still persisted, as of course it does today, but its social purpose was changing as colleges and universities, especially the large new land-grant schools, filled up with working-class young men aspiring to professional jobs in the burgeoning industrial capitalism of the gilded age. Instead of just helping young men of the privileged classes to master their own class culture, colleges were now providing young men of the lower classes access into this culture so they could climb out of their own class. Thus in 1895, a professor at the University of Minnesota explained that the study of rhetoric and literature may be of great help to "a boy" who "may lead his class in mathematics and Latin and chemistry and still be unable to free his tongue from the Scandinavian accent, or his written work from foreign idioms."[4] But much higher claims were made for the study of literature, and late nineteenth-century professors of English were full of high-flown Arnoldian

ideals about how their discipline ennobled, enlightened, uplifted, broadened, deepened, and generally "cultivated" the
mind, the spirit, and even the soul. Those of us who have spent
much time in meetings of English departments would of course
have to agree that the serious study of literature certainly does
create human beings with deep minds, uplifted spirits, and
noble souls.

Looking through this inflated language to its core of practical meaning, we can see that the study of literature was primarily a means for students to become acculturated into the
class to which they aspired. And it was therefore a means for
its professors to have a professional function in the new political economy. Since literature had the magical power to accul-
turate people into a higher class, some academic authorities still
persisted in arguing the opposite side of the same coin, maintaining that its study must be restricted to a relative elite, for
otherwise the bulk of the population would be unfitted for
their lower social functions. This argument had been heard in
America for decades, having been used to outlaw literacy for
Blacks and to combat free public education. Here is an example
from 1830, a plea against public schools:

> Literature cannot be acquired without leisure, and wealth gives lei-
> sure. . . . The "peasant" must labor during those hours of the day which
> his wealthy neighbor can give to the abstract culture of his mind;
> otherwise, the earth would not yield enough for the subsistence of all:
> the mechanic cannot abandon the operations of his trade for general
> studies; if he could, most of the conveniences of life and objects of ex-
> change would be wanting; languor, decay, poverty, discontent would
> soon be visible among all classes.[5]

The triumph of industrial capitalism, with its demands for a
more or less literate working class, cut most of the ground out
from under these arguments, at least until they were revived in
the decaying stages of the capitalist economy. At the turn of
the century they were applied to another group entering the
hallowed groves of academe: women. In 1904, a university

president thus explained how higher education interferes with the proper social function of women: "It is now well established that higher education in this country reduces the rate of both marriage and offspring. . . . I think it established that mental strain in early womanhood is a cause of imperfect mammary function which is the first stage of the slow evolution of sterility."[6] And here we have a scientific article, published in 1905, entitled "Higher Education in Women":

> Not only does wifehood and motherwood not require an extraordinary development of the brain, but the latter is a decided barrier against the proper performance of these duties. . . . The duties of motherhood are direct rivals of brain work, for they both require for their performance an exclusive and plentiful supply of phosphates. These are obtained from the food in greater or less quantity, but rarely, if ever, in sufficient quantity to supply an active and highly educated intellect, and, at the same time, the wants of the growing child. . . in this rivalry between the offspring and the intellect how often has not the family physician seen the brain lose in the struggle. The mother's reason totters and falls, in some cases to such an extent as to require removal to an insane asylum . . . most of the generally admitted poor health of women is due to over education, which first deprives them of sunlight and fresh air for the greater part of their time; second, takes every drop of blood away to the brain from the growing organs of generation; third, develops their nervous system at the expense of all their other systems, muscular, digestive, generative, etc; fourth, leads them to live an abnormal single life until the age of twenty-six or twenty-seven instead of being married at eighteen, which is the latest that nature meant them to remain single; fifth, raises their requirements so high that they can not marry a young man in good health.[7]

Here, in an extremely sharp form, we have a presentation of the social theory underlying one of the most crucial and sacred beliefs of our profession, the radical split between body and mind. Utterly beyond the conception of this dichotomized vision is the notion that the physical experience of being a woman, or a slave, or a worker, of an African would itself be the source of intellectual activity, ideas, understanding. Although the battle to exclude women from higher education was soon defeated, literature espousing the equality of women was excluded for decades. Can you imagine a literature course in the opening years of the twentieth century presenting, say, Kate Chopin's *The Awakening*? No, that was another task that was to remain for the 1960s. So just as working-class people were trained in literature courses to see themselves through literature created mainly by another class, women were trained to see themselves through literature created mainly by the opposite sex.

Tracing our understanding of the class biases built into the very structure of American higher education leads inevitably back to Thorstein Veblen's classic *The Higher Learning in America,* published in 1918, several years after he was fired from his associate professorship at Stanford University. Veblen rigorously demonstrated that our colleges and universities had become instruments of corporate capitalism, controlled both directly and indirectly by the capitalist class, internally dominated by what he labeled, with his characteristic wit, "the captains of erudition," and that, for these very reasons, the ideational core of each academic discipline had been rigidly shaped to support the capitalist structure.

But powerful contrary social forces were already in operation. After World War I and the Russian Revolution, the definition of literature changed radically—mostly outside the academy but partly within it as well. The 1920s and 1930s saw: the Harlem Renaissance, the discovery of the great mass of American popular and native literature, the development of proletarian theories of literature, and conscious groups of working-class authors. By the early 1930s, anthologies of American literature often included generous selections of native American poetry, Negro spirituals and blues, ballads and work songs, folk tales, and other forms of popular literature. The most widely used anthology of poetry, for example, was Louis Untermeyer's *American Poetry from the Beginning to Whitman* (New York: Harcourt, Brace and World, 1931) and the second volume, *Modern American Poetry* (New York: Harcourt, Brace and

World, various editions through the 5th, 1936). The first volume included examples and analyses of the earliest Afro-American poetry, plus sections entitled American Indian Poetry; Spanish-Colonial Verse; Early American Ballads; Negro Spirituals; Negro Social, "Blues" and Work-Songs; "Negroid" Melodies; Cowboy Songs and Hobo Harmonies; Backwoods Ballads; and City Gutturals. The second volume contained generous selections from such Black poets as James Weldon Johnson, Paul Laurence Dunbar, Claude McKay, Jean Toomer, Langston Hughes, and Countee Cullen. These Black poets were generally considered important figures in our literature, as one can see by examining other widely-used anthologies, such as Alfred Kreymborg's *Lyric America: An Anthology of American Poetry, 1630–1930* (New York: Coward-McCann, 1930) and *The New Poetry: An Anthology of Twentieth-Century Verse in English,* edited by Harriet Monroe and Alice Corbin Henderson (New York: Macmillan, 1932).

But during this same period there emerged a group of critics, originally coalescing at Vanderbilt University, who frankly proclaimed themselves "reactionaries" and who dedicated themselves to purging the literature of poor and working people from what was to be studied and taught. Their announced purpose, spelled out in *I'll Take My Stand* (1930) and *Reactionary Essays* (1936), was to separate literature from its social context and to combat the "vulgar" culture of industrial America, promulgating in its place the "finest" values of "the Old South," some precious, archaic literary forms that would be as irrelevant as possible to most people's lives (such as seventeenth-century metaphysical poetry), and a select handful of modern authors (notably themselves and such equally reactionary figures as T. S. Eliot). They immediately began churning out anthologies intended to make their values dominant in the teaching of literature.

Then came World War II and its sequel, the sweeping repression of the late 1940s and early 1950s. During this period, New

Criticism became the dominant critical methodology, and the anthologies compiled by the New Critics redefined the literature to be studied. Probably few of the professors who had survived the 1947–1953 purges thought of themselves as political ideologues. When they were choosing from within the canon the handful of "masterpieces" they were going to require their students to read, or when a few of them constructed their own anthologies, they probably did not think of themselves as making selections and rejections based on criteria congenial to their own social class. But by the mid 1950s, almost the entire body of literature created and widely enjoyed by the peoples of America had been rejected in favor of an infinitesimal canon of "great" works by literary "masters," mostly professional white gentlemen not unlike those selecting them. All this is thoroughly documented in my book *The Victim as Criminal and Artist,* where I show, for example, that by the early 1960s the American literature taught in our colleges and universities, collected in our academic anthologies, and discussed in our literary histories was just as lily-white as the faculty club at Johns Hopkins or Stanford.

So it was against the dominance of these theories of literature, and departments structured to implement them, that the rebellion of the 1960s aimed its polemics. For those activists at the 1968 Modern Language Association convention had begun to understand the connection between what was happening in the classroom, the department meeting, the anthology, the literary history, even the convention itself, and those other events of 1968, in the ghettoes, in Vietnam, in the political conventions, and in the streets around them.

The history of the subsequent decade is familiar to most of us, though even the few of us who are here might have many disagreements about what exactly has happened. There are two things we might all agree about, however. One is that the range of literary studies has broadened considerably, to include literature of nonwhite peoples, science fiction, detective literature, oral literature, women's studies, film, children's literature, and even some of the much-abused proletarian literature of the 1930s. We may have different opinions about whether this is good, but we can hardly disagree that it is happening, for our program here at the English Institute began with a very important session on literature excluded from the canon of the 1950s and early 1960s—the literature of Third World peoples. The second fact we would probably all agree about is that in the last several years there has been a counterattack against the beachheads established in the late 1960s and early 1970s, carried out under the authority of alleged economic exigencies and under the banner of "back to basics."

If this counterattack from the past succeeds, it will be quite destructive. For the belletristic dogma of the great tradition cannot possibly win either the students or the funds necessary for the survival of literature departments, which could conceivably be reduced to what they were a century ago: service departments for students being groomed for careers in technology, bureaucracy, and business. The alternative is for literature departments to abandon their suicidal elitism and to teach literature that is, in one way or another, relevant to the lives of the great masses of people, and to teach it in ways that these people can perceive as relevant. I have used the term *relevant* quite deliberately, because I am well aware that it now triggers a negative response among many people in our profession, and I want those people in this room who had this response when I used the word to think about it. For when relevant becomes a dirty word in our profession, then our profession may be well on its way to making itself entirely irrelevant.

Well, someone might ask, What does this have to do with class biases? And what in the world do you mean by relevant? The dominant class bias is still toward the feudal and bourgeois world views projected in the literature of the great tradition, world views that are becoming increasingly archaic. Now here I want very much not to be misunderstood. I am not saying we should throw out the literature of the past. (In fact, all extant literature was created in the past.) I am saying we should not present any literature as though it were divorced from actual human time, nor should we present it as a means of subtly propagandizing the interests of our own social class. The literature of the great tradition is a minute part of the literature of the past, and most of its value may come from its preservation of outlooks that are indeed archaic. To be relevant, the study of literature must relate in some understandable way to the following realities:

We people of the twentieth century are living through the most profound changes in human history. Our time and our space have been transmuted by such now mundane contrivances as the automobile and the airplane, electric power grids and electronic computers, radio and television. We have had world wars and decades of global revolution. We have become capable of flight beyond our own planet. We twentieth-century human beings have an emerging sense of ourselves as a single species trying to control its destiny on a minor planet in an incomprehensibly vast universe.

Our new technology has allowed us to peer deeply into the macrocosmic and microcosmic dimensions of that universe. A general theory of this material universe has been developed. We seem to have verified that theory experimentally, releasing inconceivable energy from the forces that constitute matter, and we have observed and measured events hypothesized in that theory, including astronomical occurrences from several thousand million years back in time and radiation released within a second or two of the primeval fireball that is now thought to have generated our universe perhaps fifteen to twenty billion years ago.

We have manufactured weapons capable of destroying our species, and we have developed productive resources capable of satisfying all the material needs of our species. The relations between the sexes are being radically transformed by the changing material conditions of existence. Some of the most visionary dreams of the nineteenth century now seem possibly attainable within the lifetime of some people alive today: political and economic equality between women and men, and between white and nonwhite peoples; a doubling of the average life expectancy and nearly universal literacy on this planet; human beings walking on another planet. Nightmares almost beyond the imagination of the nineteenth century also seem possible, including universal destruction through biological, chemical, or nuclear agents released accidentally or deliberately. As the ever-accelerating pace of scientific and technological development has constantly revolutionized the material conditions of existence, social and political upheavals have turned this into the century of global revolution—political, economic, social, and cultural.

This global revolution shapes the central contradictions of our profession and defines its essential crisis. We will not flourish, and perhaps we will not even survive, if our dominant tendency is to escape into an ever more baroque and impenetrable formalism, aping the mythical ostrich by sticking our heads into the sand and chatting with each other about the structural arrangements of the grains.

If we who study and teach literature wish that our profession survive, we must adjust our vision to a world in which most people are nonwhite, over half are female, the overwhelming majority are workers, and all live in a time of transformation so intense that it may constitute a metamorphosis.

NOTES

1. Sheila Delany, "Up Against the Great Tradition," in *The Politics of Literature: Dissenting Essays on the Teaching of Literature,* eds. Louis Kampf and Paul Lauter (New York: Random House, 1972), p. 315.

2. Ibid., p. 314.

3. Richard Ohmann, *English in America: A Radical View of the Profession* (New York: Oxford University Press, 1976), p. 247.

4. Ibid., p. 249.

5. "An Argument against Public Schools," *Philadelphia National Gazette,* July 10, 1830, quoted in Edgar W. Knight and Clifton Hall, *Readings in American Educational History* (New York: Appleton-Century-Crofts, 1951), p. 664.

6. Stanley Hall, president of Clark University. Ibid., p. 722.

7. I am indebted to Professor Joan Hedrick for these quotations from A. L. Smith, "Higher Education of Women," *Popular Science Monthly* 66 (1905), pp. 467, 469.

Diana Hume George

Stumbling on Melons:
Sexual Dialectics and Discrimination
in English Departments

> If one is to accept both the general rhetoric and the specific denials, one would have to conclude that the male academic establishment is, indeed, opposed to discrimination, but that such discrimination just does not exist. A very unlikely pair of circumstances. What is far more likely is that the male establishment has no intention of voluntarily recognizing or ending discriminatory practices that are advantageous to the members of that establishment. On the theory that the louder and longer one denies, the more truth there will be to the denial, the male establishment in higher education continues to attempt to discredit complainants with talk of illegal quotas, impending mediocrity, and reverse discrimination without ever openly stating that the real fear is equal opportunity for women.
>
> —Joan Abramson, *The Invisible Woman*

Mary Ellen Chase left the University of Minnesota in 1926 because she "was forced to acknowledge that a full or even an associate professorship in English would probably be denied [her] on the ground of [her] sex."[1] At the close of the seventies, we seem to have come far in our efforts to end sexual discrimination in our profession. Any of us could be pardoned for not realizing that women's positions in academe are increasingly rather than decreasingly vulnerable; it seems to many men that they, rather than women or minorities, are now the vulnerable group. Available statistics actually show our profession to have made very modest gains in controlling entrenched sexism, so it is somewhat peculiar that many of us are weary of the whole matter.[2] Affirmative Action horror stories about the man who didn't get the job because "they had to hire a woman" might lead anyone to think that women are overrunning the profession. Considering the formal litigation and legal status now granted to the backlash, one could assume that the whole thing has gone too far. And given the vocally expressed good wishes of what I perceive to be the majority of men in our profession, a private kind of "good faith," one wonders just where and who the bad guys are. Are they just administrators? Is it the bureaucracy? The budget crunch? Or is it simply the inevitable way-things-areness of things? Those explanations clearly do not account for the pervasiveness of sexual discrimination in the profession. Something more than passive compliance with the way things are keeps things the way they are.

The comments and conjectures that follow are not intended to apply to all men in our profession. Personal good faith cannot be precisely gauged, and all male readers will have to judge for themselves whether or not my comments apply to them. The white male backlash against Affirmative Action for women evidences the resentment and frustration of the few men who have been directly involved; but the rest of the male establishment may silently share that frustration. Male resentment toward women in the teaching profession has been forced underground by the pressure of social and academic feminism, and by legislation. As with any other set of complex and unlegislatable feelings, forcing such resentments into a state of repression does not eradicate them; it only makes them more subtle, less easily identifiable. How did this state of affairs come about?

Except at a few bastions of matriarchy, male professors of English in their forties and above were relatively free of the somewhat disturbing, even if enlivening, presence of women as their professors, fellow graduate students, and colleagues. A few of those men may have had several female colleagues and teachers; many more will remember a frightfully inspirational female high school teacher, perhaps, or that one woman who taught Victorian literature in their undergraduate years. But for the most part, the worlds of labor and love were safely divided for men who are now in their forties and older, who grew to professional maturity in a world largely without women to

contend with as superiors or as colleagues. Consider the college
song of my own institution, the Pennsylvania State University,
which was changed only very recently:

> When we stood at boyhood's gate,
> Shapeless in the hands of fate,
> Thou dids't mold us, Dear Old State,
> Into men!
> Into men!

As Jessie Bernard points out in *Academic Women,* it is
ironic that the academic institution is perceived as alma mater,
a shapeless and mystical woman.[3] Safely maternal to the extent that she is female at all, alma mater encourages to a highly
rarefied degree what all mothers must encourage in their sons,
in order that they might be molded "into men": a renuncia-
tion of the mother as sex object, and an internalization of the
authority of the father as superego. Both of these forces, maternal and paternal, institutional and familial, insist on the all-
important activity of sublimation. And there is certainly no
clearer embodiment of the sublimation process than the activity
we still call higher education. This is not to say that men's
minds in the academy are not normally occupied with sexuality. But sexuality is a pull in the opposite direction from
studying Eliot. The unity of sexual and intellectual energy is a
productive ideal, and the breach between them is one we might
all work to heal. But it is a breach, and high intellectual activity,
as we have defined it in the western world, takes place in that
breach. Making love is not likely to help you write that book on
Elizabethan love sonnet cycles, even if it should.

   Growing up in the operational model that artificially, or even
necessarily, dualizes intellectual activity and sexuality was, I
think, significant for many men now in their professional ma-
turities who are trying to cope with women as colleagues and
superiors. Women have begun to enter our profession in increasing numbers, and we are making increasing demands. The

situation is openly tense, and some men are uncomfortable to find that ". . . 'twas beyond a Mortal's share / To wander solitary there." I do not see how any of us, men or women, could have expected any of the rest of us to weather such a basic shift in the sexual politics of professionalism without considerable friction. Men in the humanities, perhaps especially in literature, are in a special position that is complicated by still other factors. At the same time that male English professors often fancy themselves conservative in upholding high standards, they are also very often proud of upholding another tradition—that of liberalism. Men in another profession might have been able to express openly their disgust with women's invasion of their private domain. But many English professors are called upon by their old-line liberalism to eschew such disgust. They were, and are, bound by what they conceive to be their egalitarianism, broad-mindedness, and commitment to healthy societal change, to repress frustrations about women entering academe in significant numbers.

If the academy was, until recently, as Father Walter Ong has contended, an arena of formalized male ritual combat in a state of historical decay, then the fragments of such ritual that men can keep become doubly significant—even, or perhaps especially, when denied. Faced with the need to claim sexual squatter's rights, and faced with the conflicting need to be decently liberal humanists as well, male English professors cannot be open about their ambivalences. Perhaps we all underestimate the degree of sexual tension in the profession in our effort to separate the politics of sex from sex itself. That effort often expresses itself as a denial that gender is the issue at all. Standards, politics, collegiality, economics, anything other than gender is likely to be cited as the issue.[4] We continue to obscure what I regard as a psychic fact of our professional gender politics: that many academic men think most academic women are not quite up to intellectual snuff. In my experience, most men will deny this. Men who say they do not harbor such socially backward notions as innate female inferiority are not necessarily lying; but some of them are, and I think many more may be lying even to themselves.

Let us begin with the men who are lying and who know that they are lying. Unless a man is either very gutsy or very stupid, he can no longer openly declare his sense that women are, in general, slightly less intelligent, less reasonable, and less intellectually acute than are most men with comparable education. Just ever so slightly less, perhaps; and his explanation of the difference may remain cultural rather than genetic. He could have acknowledged this reservation fifteen or fewer years ago. Perhaps he did. But he can no longer; to do so would be to ally himself with other classes of society whose basic values are anathema to the intellectual elite. Not very long ago, the elite experienced no such conflict of values if they declared that women were basically inferior to men, that their natural abilities suited them for less cerebral activities. These are, after all, established tenets of much of the literature we all teach, as feminist criticism has ably documented. That the situation has so completely reversed in such a short time is, to my mind, sufficient evidence that it cannot really have reversed in the minds of most men—and most women.

The male English professors who do still harbor consciously denigratory thoughts about women's intellectual capacities know that they had better not express them except in the privacy of their own homes and offices, and to only a few trusted colleagues and friends—also probably male. Nor is this any longer a merely moral issue; say anything denigrating about a woman colleague *as woman*, and you may find yourself in court. In any case, I think we would all agree that the time for confronting basic reservations about female intellectual capacity seems to have passed in a hurry. If some men are still choking on the dust, it is not surprising. Male academics are now forced to phrase their objections to women quite differently. They object to feminist defensiveness, and to what many of them

regard as the silliness of fussing over linguistic gender distinctions like "chairperson." (What next? Personholecover, they
suppose.) Perhaps they feel a weariness over the constant special
pleading of female academics who, if they have got the stuff,
will make it anyway. And, though not to a man, they privately
or even publicly regard feminist literary criticism as a suspect
activity, useless at worst, trivial at best. Certainly it is not in the
running for any criticism they would consider "privileging."

What often underlies these carefully selective and evasive
objections to women is something much more akin to the traditional stance than humanistic intellectuals are now permitted to
admit. Most English professors would never say anything as silly
as "women belong in the home," or "keep 'em barefoot and
pregnant and beat 'em once a week whether or not they need
it." (I must qualify that. In the privacy of his thin-walled office,
an eminent classicist was heard to repeat that "kinder, küchen,
und kirche" litany a few years ago. And I do not suppose he is
the only such man in the country.) But most academic men do
not believe such things at all. What I think many of them do
believe is much subtler.

The male English professor has indeed escaped the full force
of hatred and disgust toward women that many less sophisticated men still feel and openly demonstrate. But what would
make any of us imagine that most male English professors could
completely escape, in one short decade of enforced legislation
by government agencies buried under their own weight, the
ambivalence that men have always felt toward women? What
makes us think that women, too, could have escaped it? Most of
all, what makes us think that in the academy we could somehow be neutered, that we could regard each other only as
mind detached from body and a cultural burden of many centuries? What makes us suppose that a few basics of human
sexual psychology do not apply to us at all, or that they suddenly cease to apply the moment we walk through the doors of
the hallowed halls?

A MEASURE OF DISPARAGEMENT

In mental life nothing which has once been formed can perish.

—Freud, *Civilization and Its Discontents*

Even as psychoanalytic approaches to "reading the text" are gaining in respectability and intellectual stature, we do not readily apply Freud's theories about human sexuality to our own professional situations. I do not request credence here for every Freudian concept, but I do request whatever willing suspensions of disbelief may be necessary for accepting the following concepts on which my contentions are based:

1. Unconscious mental processes are reflected in overt and covert behaviors and motivations; i.e., consciousness is not self-referentially accountable for human behavior.
2. Sexuality is not mere genitality, by which measure most of what Freud said is patently ridiculous.
3. The *Oedipus complex,* as Juliet Mitchell and other revisionists have attempted to clarify, is a complex set of normal processes by which the individual is formally initiated into culture; or, as Freud writes it, "The beginnings of religion, ethics, society and art meet in the Oedipus complex."[5]
4. The Freudian delineation of the process and products of *sublimation* is, whatever qualifications should be placed upon it, functionally valid.

It is possible that one would not have to accept all of these concepts in order to agree with the statements I will make; but these statements are consequent upon my own acceptance of the concepts.

"Wherever primitive man institutes a taboo," Freud asserted, "there he fears a danger; and it cannot be disputed that the general principle underlying all these regulations and avoidances is a dread of woman."[6] We are not, of course, "primitive man," and I would be silly to contend that many of the respected scholars among you are running about in psychic loincloths, holding onto your flaccid organs for dear life, scared out of your wits by the devouring vagina dentata among you. But I will contend, with Freud, that "there is nothing in all this which is extinct, which is not still alive in the heart of man today," albeit in greatly metamorphosed and increasingly repressed form.[7] The taboos, regulations, and avoidances in this case are those of the academy; they are reflected in the puzzlingly energetic efforts to deny women fair representation, and in the Homeric machinations by which women are denied equal salary, promotion, tenure, and various other privileges.

What Freud called *dread* is the counterpart of denigration. The "residue of the castration complex in the man is a measure of disparagement in his attitude toward women. . . ."[8] The proportion of academic men who do still display attitudes that are primitive may be small; but in a culture where the nuclear family is the fundamental social and erotic unit, the normally socialized male declares his escape from a deeply rooted sense of female inferiority only with the kind of pride Milton reserved for Satan. He may, indeed, escape it on the conscious level. But on the unconscious level, as Dorothy Dinnerstein has ably argued, both denigration and fear of women are nearly inevitable constituents of the male psyche.[9]

Nor do I think women have escaped a sense of inferiority on the unconscious level. Their conscious sense of themselves as equal, competent, and capable, is maintained uncomfortably but functionally with what Freud wrote about normative feminine psychic development: that a woman "develops, like a scar, a sense of inferiority. . . . She begins to share the contempt felt by men. . . ."[10] I know no clearer indication of this than the justified anger of feminist women in the late 1960s, who were coming to a new sense of themselves by recognizing that they had, indeed, been enculturated to feel inferior. Again, the notion that such deep feelings could be regulated out of existence in a decade for either sex is fallacious.

Perhaps I appear to grant no credit to the power of conscious choice made by men and women, to the power of sweet reason. In fact, I do give it credit, and of the most significant kind. Our

status as bearers of the highest missions of culture partially ac-
counts for the peculiar form that sexism in the profession takes.
"No feature . . . seems better to characterize civilization than its
esteem and encouragement of man's higher mental activities—
his intellectual, scientific, and artistic achievements—and the
leading role that it assigns to ideas in human life."[11] What I earlier called our sense of mission, of moral superiority, is our
sense that we represent and protect the flower of civilization at
its highest and best.

I cannot undertake to elucidate the nature of the sublimation
process as Freud delineated it, but, for my purposes here, a few
quotations will suffice. "If the intellectual processes are to be
classified among . . . displacements, then the energy for the
work of thought itself must be supplied from sublimated erotic
sources."[12] Ideally, an aim-inhibited and redirected cathexis of
libidinal energy, if it qualifies as fully successful sublimation,
has truly accomplished the change of object, so that one could
in some respects assert that eroticism and intellection are utterly divorced. Ensuring that they remain divorced can become a
matter for considerable expenditure of psychic energy. (Blake
believed that their division into duality represented the suicidal
urge of culture.) Claims of labor and love, though mutually in-
terdependent, are also in conflict. They coexist, in spite of their
allegedly common source, in a state of fearful tension.

The sexual instincts develop certain peculiarities under the
"pressure of culture," according to Freud.

> This very incapacity in the sexual instinct to yield full satisfaction as
> soon as it submits to the first demands of culture becomes the source,
> however, of the grandest cultural achievements, which are brought to
> birth by ever greater sublimation. . . . The irreconcilable antagonism be-
> tween the demands of the two instincts . . . has made man capable of
> ever greater achievements, though, it is true, under the continual men-
> ace of danger . . .[13]

That danger, one that is felt most acutely by intellectual men, is
made manifest by women. If one gives the barest credibility to

the theories under discussion here, the intellectual male's reasons for wishing to preserve the divisions between labor and love become not just understandable, but perhaps inevitable.

I realize that I may seem to say that academic men need to keep women out of the academy because, if women are present, men will be under "continual menace of danger" from all the luscious female bodies which will distract them from their search for beauty and truth, from their search for punctuation variants in successive manuscript versions of a Keats ode, from their attempt to write the definitive biography of Cowley, or from their efforts to play Derrida to their own mentor's Foucault. But I do not mean that, any more than Freud meant that a man must stand in a cold shower in order to give birth to an idea. These processes are subtle, and if the antagonism Freud speaks of is deeply sublimated, sexual tension per se will not be the issue. Rather, the ambivalence of men toward women will have become, as purely as it can be, a matter of reservations about female intellectual capacity. And those reservations may be further repressed into a sense of general uncomfortableness. The intellectual man's discomfort with women in his marketplace undergoes far more intricate processes of removal from its genesis than are necessary for the hard-hat on the streetcorner who can still express his desire and disgust so directly that no women, and few men, could mistake it. But that sense of discomfort has a natural source, and there is a great deal at stake.

What is at stake is not just the division of labor and love, or the fragments of male bonding patterns, though those stakes are high enough. Rather, they are representative of issues that may be intimately connected with the very nature of knowledge in the Western world. The academy is a male preserve that has been threatened by women for a much longer time, and for much more significant reasons, than the previous discussion suggests. We are, perhaps, in the advanced rather than in the beginning stages of the struggle between men and women in academe. I have elsewhere objected to Father Walter Ong's ideas about the masculine/feminine dialectic in our profession. Here, however, I will enlist the portion of Father Ong's argument with which I concur. To my knowledge, Ong's article, "Agonistic Structures in Academia: Past to Present," is the only historical reading of sexual dialectic in educational history that takes the dialectic to be immensely significant. Published in different forms in both *Daedalus* and *Interchange,* Ong's article examines agonistic structures in the "all-male world of earlier academia," and finds that they resulted from "a disposition to organize the subject matter itself as a field of combat, to purvey, not just to test, knowledge in a combative style."[14]

The agonistic tradition, clearest in the discipline of formal logic, was "deeply rooted already in Greek antiquity. It persisted not merely through medieval dialectic and disputation, and Renaissance scholarly polemic, but with remarkable vigor well into the eighteenth century . . . and with still significant strength in certain sectors even into the mid-twentieth century."[15] The early roots of Western academicism are, according to Ong, oral and noetic, and are easily identifiable in the dialectical procedures of the Socratic dialogues. Ong follows the transformations of the agonistic style through major cultural movements, where, with complications resulting from the increasing significance of the written word, the humanist revival of classical antiquity "gave renewed life to the ancient rhetorical (oral) ideal," such that universities remained "filled with disputation and declamation" as a way of incorporating knowledge into the student. Orality in higher education remained in "more or less heavy residue throughout the nineteenth century, and . . . in some places even until the 1960's."[16] The agonistic tradition was connected with the fifteen-hundred-year history of learned Latin, which by the Renaissance was well established as a sex-linked language used only by males, and so served as a kind of tribal language that became an instrumental puberty rite for young males. Learning Latin "took place in the physical hardship setting typical for puberty rites," and "normally entailed physical punishment." The "tribal wisdom purveyed in academia" could be gained *only* through Latin.[17]

In the mid-nineteenth century, women's colleges were formed in the United States, followed by limited admission of women in all-male schools in the late nineteenth century, and, finally, "by the large-scale presence of women students in a vastly increased number of women's colleges and on still more co-educational campuses." The entrance of women into higher education "everywhere marked the beginning of the end of agonistic structures." Father Ong describes in detail the decline of Latin as required subject and as medium of instruction, the decline of the thesis method of teaching, of oral disputations and examinations, and of physical punishment. If agonistic structures were merely an interesting historical phenomenon in higher education, they would still be significant enough to indicate that even present-day male academics come out of an influential tradition that has always styled itself as ritualistic, male, and combative. Ong finds that agonistic structures were "conspicuously decadent already a century ago," and clearly "moribund or vestigial, though clearly discernable, by the end of World War II."[18] But what remains of such structures—and I think there is more left than Ong does—becomes dearer in dotage.

Father Ong attributes more than casual significance to the phenomena he is examining. "Agonia lies at the heart of the evolution of consciousness," he asserts, and "agonistic elements in academia are entangled with the dialectic of masculine and feminine."[19] As phenomena where the conscious and the unconscious meet, such ceremonial rituals within a sexual dialectic will partly determine the shape and direction of consciousness. I am uncertain about the validity of Father Ong's less verifiable conjectures, such as this last one. And I strongly disagree with Ong's further interpretations of the historical data he has uncovered. But I do agree that, when agonistic structures became weakened by the increasing presence of women, the organization of knowledge and learning was also affected, and men showed, as they continue to show, discomfort with whatever changes are implied. Our profession's nostalgic notions of defending "high standards" and "dying traditions" are at least partly based on gender issues.

Father Ong deals entirely with the entry of women into academe on the student level. I am dealing with the next inevitable step in that evolution: the entry of women on the professorial level. The ante has been upped considerably. A literature professor in his forties or older may have had many female students for a long time—often bright, often adoringly acolytic. His own superficial stereotypes may long ago have been defeated by some of his best and brightest, who may have been female. But that is, after all, a different matter from dealing with significant numbers of female colleagues. When a promotion and tenure committee sits in judgement on a female who is, by all official measures, qualified for promotion and tenure, and when her publication record and professional qualifications are as good as, or better than, theirs, and when they turn her down, as was the rule rather than the exception until very recently, they are protecting the final vestiges of a deeply patriarchal system. They are protecting against the loss of exclusivity, power, and privilege that attends all large-scale democratizations; and they are also protecting interests that have everything to do with gender. As in several ongoing cases, they are protecting something nebulous that they cannot define, but which they call by such names as *collegiality*.[20] Pressed to define it, they discover they cannot, except by facing—and that they cannot legally do—its genesis in their dread and denigration of women.

THE MILTONIC IDEAL

Among unequals what society
Can sort, what harmony or true delight?
                                        —Milton, *Paradise Lost*, Book VIII

Now I will discuss a paradigm which, though it will not apply exclusively to male academics in literature, is delineated with the scholar and teacher of literature in mind. I have called a certain kind of humanities intellectual both conservative and liberal: dedicated to rationality and yet the unwitting product of his irrationality; protective of the traditional values his discipline upholds, and also open to healthy social change. The habits of mind and language which, as I see it, most often fit the male who is ambivalent about women in academe are reflected in a specific literary model. Milton provides a paradigm for what I see as the basic structure of relations between men and women in academe, and specifically in literature. The male academic's dilemma in the area of sexual/professional politics is very like Milton's own ambivalence regarding the ideal relationship between man and wife, and between masculine and feminine principles. I am aware that I draw an analogy between a personal/erotic relationship and a professional one that is theoretically nonerotic. I hope to have earned the right to do this by detailing the repressed erotic content of academic sexual discrimination. Perhaps, after all, I should not apologize for bringing up incompletely sublimated sexuality. Academe is a pretty sexy arena. Consider Jessie Bernard's quotation of an academic man about an academic woman:

> There she stands. A beautiful woman. Above her neck she is talking about the most abstruse subject. From the neck down her body is saying something altogether different. She wears good clothes. They show her body off to good advantage. And yet she acts as though she were completely unconscious of it. She acts as though she were a man, like the dog who thinks he is a human being. Sometimes it strikes me as

almost freakish, this split between the way she talks and the way she looks. The two don't go together. Which message am I supposed to be getting?[21]

Like Adam and Milton's narrator in *Paradise Lost,* neither of whom seem able to take their eyes off Eve's unfallen body even though both wish to love her as a rational being, some academic men probably do feel as though "the two don't go together." As women enter academe in larger numbers, many of the changes effected are as profound as those wrought in Adam's life by Eve's creation in *Paradise Lost.* Adam's difficulties and pleasures reflect not only those of Christian man throughout history, but especially those of his author—Milton, not God, though one could argue that it comes to much the same thing.

Milton expected more from relationships between men and women than most of his counterparts in literary history. Intellectual capacity, far from being an unlooked-for adornment, was an absolute attribute of his ideal woman. In the divorce tracts, Milton detailed his idea of the true marriage as one of minds, and he adumbrated that ideal in the prelapsarian scenes of *Paradise Lost.* The true marriage was to be preserved in "love and reason." Meet help, for Milton, meant "conformity of disposition." Fitness resides in "unity of mind;" thus God promises Adam "another self, a second self, a very self itself." True love proceeds from what Milton called "intellective principles," without which there is no love because there is "nothing rational."[22]

Many of the sentiments expressed in *The Doctrine and Disciplines of Divorce* are perhaps genuinely misogynistic, but just as many are comparatively feministic. (Feminists who would toss out Milton make as great a mistake as those who reject Freud.) Lack of emphasis on intellectual communion in clerical texts and courtesy books alike in the seventeenth century reinforced the widespread assumption that bonds of rational affection with a woman are irrelevant because they are impossible. Milton attacked those honored assumptions; woman could and should be man's fit intellectual companion, for she is a human being possessed of right reason.

Existing simultaneously with these radical ideas of sexual dialectic, and apparently disturbing those ideas not at all, are Milton's firm and conventional assumptions of basic, irremediable feminine inferiority. His sources, sacred and secular, suggested no other possibility. Almost uniquely in literature, Milton's ideas enact that Freudian "measure of disparagement," which even the right-minded man cannot escape; Milton's historical context has a psychic counterpart which, if not ahistorical, is so broadly historical that it encompasses modern human history in the West. Milton's delineation of the ideal in *Paradise Lost* consequently retains basic female inferiority with Pauline conviction, while at the same time insisting that virtue in woman is a function of reason. Woman's pretense to intellectual parity was for Milton exactly that: a pretense, a misguided assumption of capacity beyond, though only just beyond, her actual limitations. Milton's idea of the small but crucial distance between man's and woman's intellectual abilities is demonstrated in his judicious phrasings in *Tetrachordon*. Man is not to hold his wife as a servant, "but receives her into a part of that empire which God proclaims him to, though not equally, yet largely, as his own image and glory." For "it is no small glory to him that a creature so like him, should be made subject to him."[23]

"A creature so like him." How like him did Adam want Eve to be? How like him did Milton want Mary Powell to be? Milton's own confusion is represented in *Paradise Lost* by interactions between Adam and the voice of the Divine Presence. In the playful banter in Book VIII, Adam expresses his frustration about being alone, except for the animals, thus: "Among unequals what society / Can sort, what harmony or true delight?" The Presence answers:

What next I bring shall please thee, be assured.
Thy likeness, thy fit help, thy other self,
Thy wish exactly to thy heart's desire.[24]

Thy wish exactly: Adam's wish is for his equal, and it will be
for mistaking her as that—the fulfillment of the promise of
God—that Adam falls. Milton's God lied to Adam, and perhaps implicitly to Milton. Although both were apprised of the
fine print afterward, both held that ideal of equality in mind.
Eve is created, and Adam is smitten. She is "bone of my bone,
flesh of my flesh, my self . . ." (VIII, 495). She is his equal as
he apprehends it at the time, his other half, his very self.

But "my self" will share all my opinions, of course, and my
"fit help" will help me. The contradictions conflated in these
few quotations from *Paradise Lost* are the contradictions inherent in an ideal that tries to combine equality with "likeness."
Milton, like his Adam, desired "fellowship . . . fit to participate/
All rational delight." (VIII, 389–91) But indeed, "among unequals what society can sort, what harmony or true delight?"
The wish for preeminence and authority makes Adam's and Milton's other wish, for equality, impossible to fulfill. How have an
unequal equal? By logic chopping, of course, by nice distinctions
in degree and kind, which order one's universe. Unlike the
Greeks, unlike the medievals, unlike even the Renaissance son-
neteers with the possible exception of Spenser, Milton's own
naked contradictions express those of the modern intellectual
male. The male in our profession who is ambivalent about women
is certainly not content with a basic paradigm for male/female
relationships which leaves him without fit help to participate in
rational delight. He wants her equal, he wants her submissive,
he wants her very bright indeed, and he believes her to be—but
he doesn't want her to be too bright, please, not bright enough
to fulfill his other wish and fear, that for genuine equality. For
if a woman is perceived as genuinely equal in intellectual capacity, then a man—all men—can hardly expect that she will remain
content with passive submission, with sharing his opinions.

In the traditional interpretation of the temptation scene in
Paradise Lost, the serpent appeals primarily to Eve's vanity, for
which we have been prepared by the text. She should be seen
and appreciated by many men, says the serpent. "Into the
heart of Eve his words made way" (IX, 55). But the confronta-
tion between Eve and the serpent occupies some two hundred
and fifty lines, of which a bare twenty-five are devoted to such
appeals. The greater part of the temptation is based on the desire for knowledge and wisdom. This is the Miltonic woman's
real subversion, the desire to know rather than to be merely
admired. It appears that this is the deepest fear of man, and of
Milton. It represents not only the revolt of humanity against
God, but the literally analogous one, in Milton's own terms, of
woman against man.

Eve's internal monologue as she struggles to make her decision
makes no mention at all of her desire to be bodily admired.
Like the "freakish" academic woman who so confused the man
I quoted above, Eve is rather concentrating on this "intellectual
food." This is finally Eve's fall, into mind above body. It is all
meant, of course, to be wrong reasoning. But in a vitally biblical
sense, it is nothing of the kind. The tree of the knowledge of
good and evil yields real fruit in the scriptural account.

> And the Lord God said, Behold, the man is become as one of us, to
> know good and evil: and now, lest he put forth his hand, and take
> also of the tree of life, and eat, and live forever. . . .
>
> (Genesis 3:22)

The Genesis God is unabashedly threatened by humanity's
potential to "become as one of us." Following Milton's own
analogy, "he for God only, she for God in him," the import
of the temptation scene becomes clear. Adam, Milton, and
God all are threatened by the possibility of woman's intellectual
equality, even as they wish for something close to it in degree.
Sex and power are the major themes of *Paradise Lost,* and the
power issue is as much between man and woman as between
humankind and God, or good and evil.

The nature of the political emphasis is accentuated in Eve's attempt to decide "in what sort" to appear to Adam. She considers keeping her new-found knowledge for herself. Shall she

> . . . keep the odds of knowledge in my power
> Without copartner? so to add what wants
> In female sex, the more to draw his love,
> And render me more equal, and perhaps,
> A thing not undesirable, sometime
> Superior; for inferior, who is free?
>
> (IX, 820-5)

Her words hearken back, with unintentional irony, to Adam's own statement in converse with God before Eve's creation. What harmony and "true delight" can occur between unequals? This is "fallen" reasoning, to be sure, partaking as it does of raw power politics. It is also the first statement that Eve is ever discontented with her subject status. The indication, however, was evident in her desire to leave Adam's side. That was unfallen Eve speaking, and this is fallen Eve. In the first instance, Eve attempted to argue that she was Adam's equal in virtue; now she admits that she is not equal, and that she wishes to be equal. The emphasis is now on power instead of volition. Fallen perception acknowledges the reality behind this other "outward show," that of an ideal relationship which glosses over intricate human difficulties. Inferior, who is free indeed?

That is the question finally asked, in the last decade, by academic Eves who have tired of the perpetual acolyte role, the dutiful-daughter role, the bright-but-not-too-bright role. And the response of many academic males has been the clearest possible embodiment of Miltonic ambivalence and self-contradiction. I call it Miltonic because the intellectual male's ambivalence is of this special kind, which is so ironically founded on the inclination to regard women as rational beings capable of participating in "all rational delight." Whether one follows the Freudian terminology of the inevitable "measure of disparagement," or the Miltonic phrasing of "She for God in him," we are speaking of the same phenomena.

The number of Milton seminars is, unfortunately, decreasing, but the Miltonic male in academia is still alive. He is the man of faith and reason, torn between conservative and radical desires. He is learned, well-versed in the classics, and acutely perceptive. But he has some predictable blind spots, and his confusion about the contradiction between his fear of woman's parity, and his desire for it, makes his a special case. The Miltonic male thinks women should be, and are, intellectually formidable. What he has trouble facing, unlike Milton, is that he still does not want women to be quite as bright as men, and does not believe that they are, and fears that they might be; fears it because woman's intellectual equality signals man's eventual demise as master in his own professional house. Woman's claims to parity of all kinds seem to him as do Eve's: basically spurious, fundamentally unsound. Woman may possess significant intellectual dimension, but she should retain a place in the chain of being, in the still implicit hierarchy from animals to angels, a slight but respectable distance below his.

CONCLUSIONS

In numbers and in proportions, the statistical patterns indicating continued sexual discrimination in our profession are neither as dismal as they were at the beginning of the decade, nor as encouraging as we have a right to expect. I ponder that sense of righteous expectation; one is bound to be disappointed when one's expectations are dependent upon the basic conservatism of any institutional structure. Where did our sense of expectation come from? Certainly no man or woman in our profession should have achieved adulthood with the idea that the world operates on principles of fairness, decency, or merit. Perhaps humanities professionals of both sexes can plead occupational insanity for their continued expectation that things will change rapidly to accord with an ideal which nearly everyone agrees, on the conscious level, is right. Humanists do think their world, as opposed to the business world at large, should conduct itself humanely. We comfort ourselves for our economic undervaluation by assuring ourselves of a largely spurious moral superiority. We make that sense of superiority a nearly spiritual matter; we have the cheek to talk about truth and beauty, as well as those lesser gods in our pantheon: integrity, decency, and ethics. If we are the poor in filthy lucre, then we are the rich in intellectual integrity. We like to think we are not a business in an economy of other businesses. We show our reluctance to accept our status as workers by various concrete behaviors, such as resisting unionization. At their worst, these institutional tendencies in the humanities engender the hypocrisy any victim of discrimination in the profession can cite. Perhaps these sentiments also reflect the best in us. There is a legitimate sense of betrayal when a young professional, who has believed in the humaneness of the humanities, who has believed that the profession will police itself and act as its own moral enforcement agency, and who has believed that open discrimination will not be tolerated once it is known, learns that his or her faith was unfounded.

But many of these disillusioned young professionals—and I include myself here—have become passive accomplices in our own undoing, by participating in that sense of moral superiority as compensation for our economic impotence. The stance of academic feminism toward an oppressive patriarchy may be legitimate, but the us/them division is still, in part, a convenience. Anyone who has lamented the lowering of standards, from freshman comp to the Modern Language Association (MLA), is objecting not only to the alleged death of the word, but also to processes that, as I have said, attend all democratizations: loss of exclusivity, loss of privilege, loss or lowering of the place we think we occupy in intellectual history. We were all, to varying degrees, taught to think we uphold and seek some kind of truth. By the very structuring of our graduate educations, many of us learned to imagine ourselves fighters for that truth, preservers of something precious and dying. But which truth are we fighting for or preserving? Whose truth? And for whom? When do what Wallace Stevens called "supreme fictions" become, in addition to being truths about the power of the imagination, ways of lying to ourselves, of avoiding what democratization entails?

I may seem to have come far from my topic, but the problems in what we as a profession conceive to be our purposes intersect the role of sexual discrimination at every possible point. I ask the women I am addressing here, and I sense the irony in the form the question takes: what do you want? I know what I sometimes want. I want to be a full professor with tenure at a well endowed university. I want a light teaching load, able graduate students whose work reflects well on me, first-rate research facilities, and leisure provided by my ability to pull in grants—all this so that I can think noble ideas and live what I have learned to covet as our version of the good life. But do I covet the right things? Many of us, mad as hell at "them" and by god not going to take it anymore, would really rather like to be them. Not an ignoble ambition, but a problematic one. English Institute members gather because they value what is left of the vulnerable enterprise of talking together about literature in time-honored and traditional ways. I certainly value that enterprise. I style myself a liberal, and we liberals love lost causes. I love this losing cause, and I find continued value in preserving it. But I do not think it is the liberal in me that loves it. It is the conservative, in the best and worse senses, the aspect of me which, seemingly without choice, must devalue what I spend most of my time doing, which is teaching.

We all have the word now, do we not? The dean of a small college who acknowledged in an interview that teaching is irrelevant to promotion and tenure considerations was really coming clean. Official tenure and promotion regulations still pretend, at most institutions, that teaching is the first and most significant consideration. But that's a joke. Increasingly, teaching is simply nowhere at all in the hierarchy of considerations. Thoroughly wretched teaching evaluations can still be used against a person if the institution wants to get rid of him/her anyway. But for the most part, teaching is functionally irrelevant to promotion and tenure, despite all the organized fuss about objectively administered student evaluations. When women learn to play the publication game—and we play it increasingly well, because we must—we are buying into a tendency in the profession that may well be called sinister. That tendency is, along with the moral superiority myth with which it is intimately connected, the most self-destructive facet of our institutional lives. Study III of the Modern Language Association Commission on the Status of Women in the Profession, "Women in Modern Language Departments, 1972–73," details the complex ways in which the devaluation of teaching intersects sexual discrimination issues, and calls for a profession-wide reconsideration of our emphasis on scholarship and publication.[25] The conclusions of the study on these points are in no sense outdated; rather, promotion and tenure patterns in the remainder of the decade have validated its claims.

But no such reconsideration of our institutional emphases seems to be forthcoming, so academic feminism is caught in the untenable position of having to construct an old-girl network to counter the old-boy network which is, as we all know, well represented by the English Institute. Organizations such as this one should be in the process of reevaluating their emphases, their reason for being, and their participation in sexual discrimination. I have heard the English Institute referred to as a "bastion of patriarchy." In the interests of knowing my audience, I decided to determine whether or not that is a fair judgment. I was able to draw several conclusions after examining my limited sample, and I should be corrected if I have made mistakes.[26] Very few women have been asked to address the English Institute. Women are unlikely to be directors of sessions, and are even less likely to be editors of the published proceedings. When women are among the program participants, their presentations are not likely to be selected for publication, for reasons that may have little to do with gender; still, the pattern has been discouragingly clear.

That pattern is beginning to change. Whether or not it is changing rapidly enough is a matter of opinion. The English Institute's tendency to follow the pattern of the profession at large in passive omissions of proper representation of women is not necessarily deliberate.[27] The discrimination operating here requires careful definition. It certainly intersects selectivity, and the institute is not likely to feel apologetic for upholding its highly selective standards. If I understand things aright, this organization is conservative in what could be called the best sense. There is something to be said for an organization that continues to provide a forum for the best literary criticism while the rest of the profession embroils itself in political upheaval. But there is also something to be said against such a venture, because it is partly a lie. There are politics involved here, too, of a kind that the profession at large no longer views as benign. The fact that the institute is still a thing apart, an organization whose prestige is still indisputable, makes its underrepresentation of women particularly significant. Although it might appear that such a gathering of scholars is able to hold itself above petty politics and "the busie companies of men," it is widely known that a small and very busy company of men has always constituted the basic structure of the institute. And although this year's program states that it is "designed to provide fresh approaches to literary study," fresh approaches are not what the institute is known for. In an informal poll of a few dozen people in our profession, I found that some version of the term "exclusive club" is how the institute is widely regarded. The crème de la crème of the old-boy network.

How, in fact, do I come to address the English Institute at the near-beginning of a career which, right now, sees me teaching a great deal of freshman comp at an extension college of a large land grant university? Through the old-boy network, that's how. We all know that's the way it works. My old boy, though he has called himself an unregenerated Jewish patriarch, is nothing of the kind. I suppose it is suspect to call him an old boy at all. He is male, and he is getting older, but he has spent his professional life writing about, and being, another kind of outsider. Indeed, names such as Fiedler on the supervising committee mean that the institute is changing its image slowly, and I should not underestimate that change. Moreover, the topic of this group of meetings itself indicates change. But I wonder how many institute members are not entirely pleased with these tardy transformations. Even if the predominant attitudes of the institute toward feminist concerns in the profession are positive—and I think I may be pardoned for doubting that they are—they are likely to gloss over sex discrimination. I can explain what I mean only by dispensing with what little sense of propriety I have retained here and articulating what we all know.

I have repeatedly heard that giving a paper at MLA "doesn't really count anymore." And "doesn't really count" means that the MLA is becoming increasingly democratized. This means, I am afraid, that democratization is perceived by most of us, as I have said, as accompanied by a hopeless lowering of standards. "Doesn't really count" means, among other things, that the MLA is overrun by feminists, and Marxists, and gays, and radical caucuses of seemingly endless variety. The English Institute has never had radical caucuses to my knowledge. Giving a paper at the English Institute "still counts," and everyone here knows what that means. A promotion and tenure committee can discount a presentation at a feminist criticism session of MLA.

(I am sure that an automatic discount formula exists in the minds of most of us, from about 25 percent up to a rounded 100 percent.) As a woman in the profession, I must realize that my own tacit participation in any such discounting process, and my lamentations about declining standards, are tinged with irony. "This means you" is the content of those lamentations. Nothing will make a feminist academic angrier than the veiled contention that women in academe, or the concerns of feminist criticism, will result in lower standards. But they will, and they are, because "standards" is still a patriarchally defined concept.

The English Institute has a distinguished reputation to guard. If many more sessions like this one take place, the nature of the institute will irrevocably change, and such changes can legitimately be called a *lowering of standards.* It would be overly ingenuous to suppose that there will be no resistance to the process my own participation here represents. The English Institute is the most prestigious organization in our corner of academe, and it has greatly underrepresented women. The concurrence of these two facts—high prestige and low representation of women—makes the institute's form of discrimination especially significant. If the center of authority and exclusivity in the profession remains predominantly male, the politics, or religion, or ethnic identity of some of the males notwithstanding, every woman in the profession should be concerned about it.

The English Institute is indeed making good faith efforts now, and I applaud those efforts. The steering committee now includes several women, whose presence in such important positions is in itself significant. But there is a paradox here: greater representations of women will not automatically effect the transformations necessary to end the institute's identification as a bastion of patriarchy. Such transformations would require fundamental shifts in the institute's raison d'être to include not only women's concerns, but also those of blacks and Third World groups. An emphasis on teaching would, for the reasons discussed above, be more than incidental to such transformations. The institute's preeminence means, in my opinion, that it should make such efforts consciously rather than fortuitously, and repeatedly, rather than occasionally. Dispense with the fiction of political neutrality. It is silly to pretend there is no old-boy network. Rather, I ask its voluntary and increased assistance. I ask the old-boy network to deconstruct itself, and then to self-destruct.

NOTES

1. Jessie Bernard, *Academic Women* (University Park: Pennsylvania State University Press, 1964), p. 50.

2. See "Study III: Women in Modern Language Departments, 1972-73: A Report of the Modern Language Association Commission on the Status of Women in the Profession," *PMLA* 91 (1976): 124-36. Study IV is scheduled for publication in 1980 or 1981. But unless something is happening in English departments that is utterly unlike patterns in the academic world as a whole—and I have uncovered no information that would allow me to suppose this—the conclusions of Study IV are not likely to render Study III passé. In fact, Study III's predictions have been fulfilled: "The opportunities offered by the growth of education in the 1960s were lost; there will be no growth in the 1980s. Thus, unless women in modern languages are hired and tenured *at a faster rate than men* in the remainder of this decade, their present situation will be perpetuated" (p. 126). The decade has ended. Study IV may include a few surprises. But judging from current statistics for the profession as a whole, and from the trends with which English departments have corresponded over a long period of time, those surprises are not likely to be big or many. Study III argues that the profession must reevaluate its emphasis on publication in order for women to advance significantly, since the representation of women remains glaringly disproportionate at universities, where publication is encouraged by lighter teaching loads and good research facilities. "Given shrinking enrollments and the scarcity of funds, however, such changes seem unlikely to occur; rather, the Commission feels, more institutions will model themselves on the research university, where, it has been noted, the disequilibrium between men and women is greatest. This trend bodes ill for the future of women in the profession. . . ." Other trends that seem to be developing are equally harmful to the status of women in the profession. A series of new court decisions on all judiciary levels indicates, according to *On Campus with Women*, "a growing trend toward the rejection of sex discrimination claims brought by women faculty members against colleges and universities." Indicative is the *Preseisan* v. *Swarthmore College* case, in which the woman who brought charges of sexual discrimination failed to show that charges were valid because the trial court required that she show "by a preponderance of the evidence that sex discrimination against female faculty members is the standard operating procedure of Swarthmore"

(*On Campus with Women,* Project on the Status and Education of Women, Association of American Colleges, No. 20 [June 1978], p. 2). The project, directed by Bernice Resnick Sandler, provides information concerning women in education, and works with institutions and government agencies. The Spring 1979 and Winter 1979 issues of *On Campus with Women* detail specific court cases and discuss misallocations of affirmative action funding. For information on the abuse of women, minorities, and affirmative action through the misuse of adjunct faculty, see Joan Abramson, *The Invisible Woman: Discrimination in the Academic Profession* (San Francisco: Jossey-Bass Publishers, 1975), especially p. 118; Nuala McGann Drescher, "Affirmative Action: Outlook Not Sunny at SUNY," *Universitas* (December 1978), unpaginated; and Paul Lauter, "A Scandalous Misuse of Faculty: 'Adjuncts,'" *Universitas* (December 1978), unpaginated. (*Universitas* is published by United University Professions, the faculty and professional agent for the SUNY system.)

3. Bernard, *Academic Women,* p. 1.

4. Portions of the following argument are reproduced, with variations, from my article, "The Miltonic Ideal: A Paradigm for the Structure of Relations between Men and Women in Academia," *College English* 40 (1979): 864–73.

5. Sigmund Freud, *Totem and Taboo,* trans. A. A. Brill (New York: Random House, Vintage Books, 1946), p. 202.

6. Sigmund Freud, "The Taboo of Virginity," from "Contributions to the Psychology of Love," trans. Joan Riviere, in *Sexuality and the Psychology of Love,* ed. Philip Rieff (New York: Collier Books, 1963, 1973), p. 76.

7. Freud, "Taboo," p. 76.

8. Freud, "Female Sexuality," trans. Joan Riviere, in *Sexuality,* p. 198.

9. Dorothy Dinnerstein, *The Mermaid and the Minotaur: Sexual Arrangements and Human Malaise* (New York: Harper and Row, 1976). It is difficult to suggest discrete sections of Dinnerstein's study, since her thesis is complexly developmental in presentation. See especially pp. 83–159.

10. Sigmund Freud, "Some Psychological Consequences of the Anatomical Distinction between the Sexes," trans. James Strachey, in *Sexuality,* pp. 188–89.

11. Sigmund Freud, *Civilization and Its Discontents,* ed. and trans. James Strachey (New York: W. W. Norton & Co., 1962), p. 41.

12. Sigmund Freud, "The Ego and the Id," in *A General Selection from the Works of Sigmund Freud,* ed. John Rickman, trans. Joan Riviere (Garden City: Doubleday, Anchor Books, 1957), p. 227. Sublimation as psychic process is, clearly, far more complicated than this statement indicates. For my own reading of Freudian sublimation processes, and some of my assessment of Freudian theory on feminine psychology, see Diana Hume George, *Blake and Freud* (Ithaca: Cornell University Press, 1980), especially Chapters 5 and 7.

13. Sigmund Freud, "The Most Prevalent Form of Degradation in Erotic Life," from "Contributions to the Psychology of Love," trans. Joan Riviere, in *Sexuality,* pp. 69–70.

14. Walter J. Ong, S.J., "Agonistic Structures in Academia: Past to Present," *Interchange* 5 (1974):1–12; abridged form printed in *Daedalus* 103 (1974):229–38. Citations here are from the *Interchange* version.

15. Ibid., p. 2.

16. Ibid., p. 4.

17. Ibid., p. 5.

18. Ibid., p. 7.

19. Ibid., pp. 7-8.

20. At the time this presentation was given the Annette Kolodny case was among the ongoing litigations in which dependence on fuzzy terminology had enabled an institution to defend itself against charges of sexual discrimination. In 1974, the English Department of the University of New Hampshire (UNH) voted not to endorse Dr. Annette Kolodny's promotion to the rank of associate professor. At the time, her book, *The Lay of the Land,* was in press, and she had four lengthy critical articles in well-respected journals, with another accepted by *Critical Inquiry.* Her credits also included numerous conference presentations and recent election to the Board of Editors of *American Literature.* The New Hampshire Commission for Human Rights found "probable cause to credit the allegation of discrimination by sex," and concluded that the English Department had "a history of non-advancement for female employees." (Kolodny was both the first woman and the first Jew in the department's entire history to be considered for a senior rank.) The commission found Kolodny's education and professional background "superior," and her teaching and scholarship "excellent." These findings were upheld at the federal level by EEOC. But UNH still did not redress Kolodny's grievances. Finally, in July 1977, she was promoted to associate professor; but in December of the same year, she was denied tenure, in spite of the Tenure Review Committee's acknowledgment of her superior teaching, publication, and service record. As this article goes to press, the Kolodny case is in the process of being settled out of court.

21. Bernard, *Academic Women,* p. 198.

22. John Milton, "The Doctrine and Discipline of Divorce," in *Complete Prose Works,* vol. 2, ed. Ernest Sirluck (New Haven: Yale University Press, 1959), p. 2.

23. John Milton, "Tetrachordon," in *Complete Prose Works,* vol. 2, p. 672.

24. John Milton, *Paradise Lost,* ed. with an introduction by William G. Madsen (New York: Random House, 1969), Book VIII, 383-84 and 449-51. Subsequent references to *Paradise Lost* are to this edition, and are designated in the text by book and line numbers.

25. "Study III," pp. 124-36.

26. The 1969-70 institute volume contains no articles by women. Of the seventeen names that comprise the officer list, two are women's. The 1970 program has no female directors and one female participant. The 1970-71 volume again includes no female contributors; there is one woman officer, one woman (out of four) session director, and either two or three women out of sixteen program participants. (It is not always possible to tell gender from names. Where there was any doubt, I included the possibility that the person might be female.) The 1971-72 volume again includes no women among those whose presentations were selected for publication; one woman officer; no female session directors; and this time, no women among the fourteen speakers. The 1972-73 volume has no articles written by women, and no women are among the officers; again, no female directors of sessions; and two female presenters out of sixteen. The 1973-74 volume is the first in my sample to include one article by a woman in the published proceedings. One woman's name appears on the officer list, but there are no female directors of sessions; the program includes either one or two female participants. In 1974-75, women again disappear as authors

of articles; one woman is among the officers, and two of the fourteen presenters are women. I was not able to examine the 1975–76 volume, and I regret that omission if it breaks what seems to be a fairly predictable pattern.

I took a close analytic look at the most recent volume I was able to examine, that for the 1976–77 program, where the institute's record is at its best. One woman's article appears in *Psychoanalysis and the Question of the Text.* Representation of women on the Supervising Committee jumps to three, and one program director is a woman; two of three panelists on her program are female. One more female program participant brings the total to three out of fifteen. To measure the fairness of this representation, I decided to use an internal yardstick. Registrants for the program are—must be—members of the institute, and thereby provide much of its substance, audience, financial support, and reason for being. Of the approximately 330 scholars registered for the 1977 program, slightly over one-third were women. Judged against that measure—one consistent, by the way, with representation of women in the profession—the one-seventh representation of women in the published volume, the one-fourth representation of women directors, and the one-fifth representation of women panelists, still constitute "underrepresentation."

27. Some of the ways in which "proper" or "fair" representation might be calculated include availability of female Ph.D.'s in the profession, by number; percentages of employed female Ph.D.'s in English departments, including those in non-continuing appointments; numbers or percentages of women holding full-time, tenure track positions; and numbers or percentages of women who have published "x" number of articles in refereed journals in their fields. I have found that any figures I consulted for a given population and time period varied slightly according to the source of data and the variables measured.

 *George Stade*

Fat-Cheeks Hefted a Snake:
On the Origins and Institutionalization
of Literature

I'd be in for an easier time of it today were it not for this dismal notion I have that institutions don't exist—materially speaking, of course. Marriage, for example, surely doesn't exist, although people exist, and some of them get married. Marrying, I mean, is to people as bouncing is to balls: balls exist, and some of them bounce, but for all the ways of handling a ball, there's no way to lay a hand on its bounce. Again: red lights exist, and cars stop at them, but though you can shoot out the light or abandon the car, there is nothing material you can do to the stopping itself, although it's what constitutes the institution. From this point of view, I regret to say, the English Institute doesn't exist either. Certainly there are people who read aloud words about other words—the words they read headed by titles with colons in them. And certainly there are listeners, or it would be foolish indeed for the readers to be reading aloud. But the English Institute is not its readers or listeners or colons, for these might be exchanged for other people, or for semicolons, without our wanting to say that the English Institute no longer is what it was, or rather wasn't. Nor is an institution a law or system of laws, for much of what goes on regularly at the English Institute is not governed by law; for although brides and grooms kiss after saying "I do," on this matter the law is silent.

To an alien intelligence, then, to an intelligence that knew neither our language nor our motives, what we call our institutions would look like a tangle of group habits. It would look as though humans had dispositions to do certain things in certain places at certain times. Our institutions would mostly look like behavior patterns activated by endogenous or environmental stimuli according to seasonal or diurnal rhythms—although habits, dispositions, patterns, and rhythms don't exist either, materially speaking. In this respect, we would look to the alien as animals look to us; for the institutions of animals don't exist in the same way ours don't, and for similar reasons.

Those reasons are evolutionary: the institutions or behavior patterns of animals fit them out for survival; so presumably did ours, once upon a time. Some behavior patterns equip an animal to survive the pressures exerted upon it by the other members of its species, its conspecifics, as biologists say. Such patterns, that is, evolved in response to intraspecific selective pressures. Pressures such as these we can fairly call social. Other patterns equip an animal to interact adaptively with everything outside of its population. Such patterns, that is, evolved in response to extraspecific selective pressures. Pressures such as these, for the sake of simplicity, we can call economic or natural, although among animals, at least, social patterns are anything but unnatural. Once any animal institutions had evolved, whether they were social or natural, they exerted selective pressures in their own right. New behavior patterns as well as new physical traits would evolve in response to them, for although institutions are immaterial, they have material consequences.

Some of these consequences are spectacular, the tails of peacocks, for example, and the equally gorgeous behinds of baboons. Neither attraction is of much use to peacocks and baboons in their struggle with nature; their function, rather, is to stimulate meaningful interpersonal relationships. So it is with the red breasts of robins, which exist strictly for the sake of other robins. So it is with the animal or human institutions made notorious by ethologists, those dominance joustings and territorial displays, those appeasement gestures and courting rites—all of which indeed have functions that are mainly social, but not necessarily the function of maintaining the society we happen now to have. So it is, less dramatically, with the red dot on the end of the herring gull's bill. When the parent gull returns from a search for food to its nest, it leans forward so that the chicks will see its bill. The chicks thereupon peck at the red dot. The parent thereupon regurgitates whatever it had been eating. It then picks up a bit of food, so that when the chicks once again peck at the red dot, they are rewarded with something to eat. The red dot is what ethologists call a social releaser: it releases the social activity of pecking, which then releases the food, so to speak. Red dot, pecking, regurgitation; social releaser and behavior pattern; physical trait and institution—these evolved in response to each other, reciprocally. They help animals get on with each other, but as a general rule what helps animals get on with each other also helps them get on in the extraspecific world around them. So it must have been with protohumans, whose institutions, like ours, are indistinguishable from behavior patterns, to the alien observer.

Protohumans, that is, presumably had protohuman institutions; they were a part of what made them protohuman. Once some of them had evolved, protohuman institutions became a part of the protohuman's environment. Like the rest of his environment, they exerted selective pressures. Behavioral and physical traits that meshed adaptively with the social or institutional environment survived and multiplied. Among such traits are an ability to visualize what is not perceptible and funny vocal cords. Maladaptive behavioral and physical traits became extinct or vestigial or suppressed, for we carry much of our pasts within us. Among such traits, we gather, were a disposition to express rage physically rather than symbolically and those stiff but powerful facial muscles that limited the protohuman's range of expressions. Protohuman institutions, on the one hand, and protohuman physical and behavioral traits, on the other, evolved in response to the pressures they exerted upon each other; they evolved reciprocally, or dialectically, like everything else, so it seems.

The notion I have been arguing against, then, is that the first human institutions were post- or transevolutionary. I have been denying that we got pretty much to where we are now physically, and only after that flew or fell into culture. To see institutions such as language and literature (neither of which, materially speaking, exist) as postevolutionary, after all, is to see them as related to the physical human as the classless society is related to history, and as the City of God is related to the other one. It is to see them as related by a leap into the absurd. The more likely alternative is that our institutions are part of what got us to where we are, physically and otherwise. It is more likely that our institutions, to begin with, functioned adaptively, whatever they do now.

Among the protohuman institutions that didn't exist, materially speaking, was the behavior pattern of storytelling. Modern anthropology, in any case, knows of no society (no matter how "primitive" it might otherwise seem to anthropologists) that is without storytellers and willing listeners—or, I might add, without critics, those second-storymen; for tribal people, like other kinds, like to comment on stories almost as much as they like to listen to them (and it is the social function of such commentary, of course, to turn stories into institutions). Storytelling, then, is a species-specific behavioral trait; at least we don't know of any other animal that tells stories, except for animals *in* stories. Storytelling is as definitively human as fully opposable thumbs and rounded buttocks, which latter, though not as gorgeous as the baboon's, have enabled us to rise above him. If storytelling had no adaptive function, it would be proof of the existence of God; it would be a miracle, a suspension of the laws of nature, the only gratuitous species-specific behavior pattern in the world. In sum, although, materially speaking, stories and storytelling do not exist, they function: they *are* functions. They are functions of our need to get on intraspecifically so that we can get on cooperatively in the extraspecific world around us.

That literature has social functions is no longer news, although storytellers often deny it. They deny it because their private interests in their stories are at odds with the institutional ones— for humans differ from animals in that the interests of the individual human, if only to the individual human, are often at odds with the interests of the group. Among such interests is the interest in stories. The private functions of literature, I am going to argue, are at odds with the institutional functions, or there would be no need for critics, whose institutional function is to coopt private subversiveness for the public interest. At the same time, it is in the public interest for private individuals to enjoy subversive fictions—just as it is in the interest of private individuals for public institutions to function, so long as they also remain adaptive. These paradoxes require evidence and instance, for which I now turn to the first story ever told.

The protohumans who invented literature lived before the great leap forward during the Paleolithic plenitude of big game protein. They were wee, timorous, and cowering, no longer able to scamper up into the safety of trees, nor yet big or cooperative or smart enough to stand off predators. They called themselves "the People," so as to distinguish themselves from other protohumans, whom they considered fair game. But most of their words were exclamatory or imperative or hortatory, signals mostly, equivalents to such things as the crow's warning caw or the baboon's amorous display of his engorged and gorgeous rump. One word, for example, might mean "Duck, there's a python at ten o'clock!" while another might mean, "Come on, baby, and knock me a kiss." Just the same, the People had syntax enough to organize exclamations and the names of things into conceptual units, into sentences. And the words they liked to organize best, the words that carried the greatest payload of emotion, were the quasi-exclamatory names of the things upon which the People depended for survival.

Their word *stake,* for example, was not the name for just any old stick. It was the name of their only implement and a man's most valuable possession, materially speaking. It was the name used for a found object of a certain length, thickness, rigidity, and toughness, good for digging up grubs and roots, for poking around in anthills and in beehives, for bludgeoning frogs and overturning porcupines. Intraspecifically, it could be used for a cane or billy club or swagger stick. Or take the People's verb *heft*, which did not mean to dandle something in the hand as though to estimate its weight. It was, rather, a technical term used solely for the act of picking up and testing a *stake*. It meant to pick up a *stake* and mime its uses, to poke, swing, shake, lean on, and swagger it. The People's Alpha male, name of Fat-Cheeks, had the best of *stakes,* and no one was his equal when it came to *hefting* one. On the whole, Fat-Cheeks was satisfied with his *stake,* his people, and himself, but he was not happy.

The impediment to his happiness was Short-Shanks, the Omega male, whose *stake* was a disgrace. It was altogether too thin, limber, crooked, and worm-eaten. It offended Fat-Cheeks's aesthetic sensibilities; it detracted from his sense of pride in the People, upon which his own self-esteem was dependent. One day, when he could stand it no longer, Fat-Cheeks broke the miserable Short-Shanks's miserable *stake* over his knee. He pulled Short-Shanks by the ear as a signal that he should come along. His intention was to find and *heft* for Short-Shanks a *stake* commensurate with the dignity of the People. Half-hidden under a thicket of brush, he saw something like what he had in mind. As much as he could see of it was thick, straight, strong-looking, a dark olive in color, nearly black. He reached down, put a hand around it, and started to *heft* it. The damned thing reared back with forked tongue, bared fangs, and a blood-curdling hiss, for this was no *stake,* but a black mamba, deadliest of serpents. Fat-Cheeks whirled the mamba once over his head, so that centrifugal force would keep the fangs away from him, and then let go. He scuttled back a few steps, tripped, and sat down hard on his fat and rounded buttocks. Short-Shanks said not a word, for Fat-Cheeks, like most Alpha males, was thin-skinned and short-tempered.

But that evening, when Short-Shanks hunkered down for a soothing session of lice hunting with his consort, name of Turtle-Neck, because that's the kind she had, he finally spoke. His momentous words were these: "Fat-Cheeks *hefted* a snake." Turtle-Neck froze, dropped the louse she was about to eat, gaped at Short-Shanks, tipped over on her back, kicked her feet in the air, and whooped with laughter, for she was jealous of the charms and privileges of Fat-Cheeks's latest consort. Only then did Short-Shanks begin to laugh, for storytellers derive their pleasures not so much from their own stories as from the imagined or material reactions of their audience. And a storyteller is what Short-Shanks had just become, the very first. "Fat-Cheeks *hefted* a snake" was the world's first work of literature.

On what grounds, you may ask, do I call this literature. How, you may want to know, does it differ from humbler sentences. After all, it doesn't look any different. Certainly I will agree that, materially speaking, there is very little to distinguish it from a sentence such as this one: "Fat-Cheeks *hefted* a *stake*" (with a *t*), which is not literature. And certainly I would agree that it is not fiction, in one sense of the word, because it is not false; when uttered, it was about as true as sentences get. I might claim, however (if I were an historical critic), that Short-Shanks's epical sentence, like all other literature, so bears the imprint of its *sitz im Leben,* like a nudist who has been sunbathing on gravel, that you can't understand it unless you know whence it arose. To understand the sentence's original meaning, at least, you would have to know something about the People, their economics and institutions, their superstitious horror of black mambas, the vortex of feelings and ideas that whirled around the words *heft* and *stake,* the social status of Fat-Cheeks and Short-Shanks and Turtle-Neck, the relations among them, the whole history of the universe until the moment of the sentence's maculate conception. But who cares about the original meaning of anything any more? Besides, you would have to know the same things to understand the original meaning of a sentence such as "Fat-Cheeks *hefted* a *stake*" (with a *t*), which, we agreed, is not literature.

Or I might claim (if I were a formalist) that Short-Shanks's epochal sentence, like any poem, is a self-contained verbal universe characterized by tension, irony, and paradox. I might point out how the swift final anapest, *ed a snake,* rears back on the lumbering trochees behind it, as the black mamba reared back on Fat-Cheeks. I might point to the gustatory pleasures of the mouth in moving from the low back vowel in "Fat-" to a high front vowel, to a middle front, to another low back, to the final low, low front vowel of "snake," never mind the laxative roughage of the consonants. I might point to the buried pun in the buried rhyme between "snake" and the absent word *stake.* But these features of the sentence do not make it literature, although they encourage us to make literature out of it. A work of literature is not a form, but a function, although its form may signal its function.

Or I might claim (if I were a Lacanian structuralist) that the sentence derives its uncanny power from the fact that the snake is all the more present for being absent; that, like all literature, the sentence recapitulates that awful moment when the little boy first saw his sister naked, only to be confronted by an absence where there should have been a presence, thus undermining his own sense of reality. Or (if I were a Derridean structuralist) I might claim that the difference between "snake" (with an *n*) and *stake* (with a *t*) reenacts the portentous difference between *difference* (with an *e*) and *differance* (with an *a*) and thus, like all literature, is a reflexive commentary on the language that comprises and compromises it. If I were an Aristotelian I would have to settle for the claim that the sentence, like all comedies, has a beginning, a middle, and an end, a doer, a doing, and a done to—unless I wanted to dwell on the cathartic qualities of the consonants. If I were an archetypal critic there would be no end to the things I might claim. All these are much-mended nets to bag literature for institutional consumption. Finally, if I were a pragmatic critic, which I am, I could claim that the sentence is a paradigm of all stories in that it is a something told by someone to someone about an absent someone else— but (if I were an aesthete) I might add, for no utilitarian purpose. If I were to add that, however, I would not be telling the truth. For the sentence does have a practical function, if not a material one, and it is that function that makes it literature. For a story, like any work of art, becomes a story or work of art by virtue of how it is used. This dark saying calls out for a short excursus.

If some dodo, for example, finds a bent and rusted Mack truck muffler in a suburban dump, and solders bottle caps on it, and displays it in a gallery; and if another dodo buys it, puts it on a pedestal in his living room, evidences pride in it, shows it to friends, who stand back to inspect it with solemn looks on their faces; and if he then wills it to a museum, so as to beat the inheritance tax—then we know that the muffler has become a work of art. Or if we see overdressed people sitting quietly in Carnegie Hall while some guy on stage tortures a whoopee cushion, or if we see the same people listening attentively to forty-eight minutes of silence while the musicians on stage, also overdressed, sit with their hands in their laps—then we know that the noise of the whoopee cushion and the forty-eight minutes of silence have become works of musical art, to the dodos that listen to them. For things that are visual, auditory, or verbal become works of art when they are used the way works of art are used by the society that considers them works of art.

Similarly, the sentence "Fat-Cheeks hefted a snake" is literature because it functioned the way what we call literature functions, because it was used the way literature is used. But it did not function in the same way for Short-Shanks and for the rest of the People. Its private and institutional functions, that is, were different; its private function, in fact, was anti-institutional, but that is how, as it turns out, it served its institutional function.

Luckily, we can recover the use to Short-Shanks of his momentous sentence, and without any recourse to depth psychology. It was used by Short-Shanks as a substitute for murdering Fat-Cheeks. Like all literature, it was a substitute in words for what the author couldn't or wouldn't do in the flesh, just as E. H. Gombrich's hobby horse was a substitute for the kind its owner couldn't afford or wouldn't want to clean up after. And like all literature, Short-Shanks's substitute was overdetermined. He acted in words rather than in the flesh because he was already so protohuman that his disposition was to express intraspecific rage symbolically rather than physically; because he partook of the institutional awe that hedges an Alpha male; because he was not sure he could bring it off; because he was not sure that if he could bring it off, he would get away with it; because he was lazy. Short-Shanks's feat was to express his anti-institutional resentment without the risk of guilt, failure, retaliation, or fatigue. And there were side benefits: the pleasure in mouthing a well-turned phrase; the admiration in Turtle-Neck's eyes; the chance that, for once, she would not repulse his amorous advances.

That's how literature functions for the individual, then, as a substitute in words for an action he can't or won't perform in the flesh. And that is in part how it serves his institutions. After suffering Short-Shanks's amorous attentions, Turtle-Neck ran off to tell his story to other women, who told it to their men. In the days that followed, many of the People used Short-Shanks's story as he had used it: to express their private resentment toward their institutional chief—but the effect was to consolidate that worthy's position. Fat-Cheeks could have censored the story, but unlike many of his successors, he was shrewd as well as strong. He was quick to notice that those of the People who repeated the story afterwards became easier in his presence, found ways of making up to him—perhaps because they were after all human enough to feel guilt over symbolic aggression, and not just the material kind. This (so far) natural process of socialization was too full of ambiguities for one of Fat-Cheeks's flunkies. He improved the original sentence with a commentary in the form of an addition. His edition of the sentence went like this:

> The least of men can heft a stake
> But only Fat-Cheeks hefted a snake.

This became the official version; when it became the only version, the institutionalization of Short-Shanks's opus was complete.

Fat-Cheeks's flunky, by the way, founded the school of criticism that looks at all works of literature as commentaries on other works of literature, and that looks at commentary as literature in itself. He later wasted away, I understand, under the anxiety of influence. But his lasting achievement was the first systematic perversion of literature for an institutional purpose, which achievement, ever since, has been the institutional function of critics. The inevitable, and adaptive, response of individuals is to deinstitutionalize. Take, for example, that dreamy-eyed protohuman girl, overweight and clumsy, a future storyteller herself, who when she heard the Authorized Version, immediately revised it into an erotic fantasy. She revised it into a fantasy of Fat-Cheeks hefting his snake for her sake alone, thereby instituting a tradition of revision faithfully honored by undergraduates ever since, much to their credit. By virtue of its availability for such usage, good literature survives institutions and their flunkies, for this is not yet the end of our story.

Once the ice had been broken, new works of literature gushed from many a sacred fount. Fat-Cheeks, for example, after driving Short-Shanks into exile (for Alpha males were protohumans as well as institutions), noticed how subdued and retiring Turtle-Neck had become. He waited for a moment of silence, cleared his throat, looked around to make sure he had everyone's attention, and in an unnaturally loud voice said this:

"Turtle-Neck has withdrawn into her shell." He thus inaugu-
rated the tradition of institutional art, which is dull because it
has no personal or anti-institutional edge.

Those of the People who followed Short-Shanks into exile
preserved the original form of the story, but they lost its
original meaning. Over millennia they became bigger from big
game protein, more cooperative through hunting it, and smarter
in response to the intraspecific pressures of their evolving language and literature. They threw away their *stakes* for a tool
kit of bone and stone. Their word "stake" now meant what it
means to us, a kind of pretentious stick. Their word "heft"
devolved to something like our "lift." Their catchphrase, "Fat-
Cheeks hefted a snake," took on the functions, pretty much, of
our catchphrase, "He walked into an exploding stove." If
Blow-Top, for example, kicked a porcupine, or Lump-Jaw
slapped at the mosquito on his ear but forgot to let go of his
stone axe first, you could count on some wiseacre to say,
"Fat-Cheeks hefted a snake."

Millennia still later, these people left their ancestral home to
escape the descendants of Fat-Cheeks's followers, who considered them fair game. They migrated north, turned the
lower right corner of the Mediterranean, and spilled into the
Near East, although it was not yet near to anything. They
learned how to tame and ragout the dogs that scavenged their
campsite detritus. They learned how to scratch out furrows,
how to plant the alien corn that had become their staple, for
big game was getting scarce thereabout. The hefty stick used
for scratching out furrows they called a *stake,* around which a
new vortex of feeling and idea began to whirl. But the first
story ever told was forgotten, except by a guild of sorcerers,
who gave it an esoteric meaning now beyond recovery. An
early scholiast, sure enough, explains that the sorcerers read
Fat-Cheeks as a synecdoche for robust health and beauty;
hefted as archaic for "plowed"; and *snake* as figurative for
"stake," for over millennia the repressed slowly returns, even

in language. The scholiast's full translation of the sorcerer's alleged meaning goes like this: "Pleasing Plumpness plied his plow," or "Through work wax wonderfully." For a long time this reading held, but a noisy group of revisionists have recently denounced it as a euphemism at best and at worst, propaganda, an attempt to reconcile workers to their chains. Thus literature evolves dialectically with the institutions that coopt it and with the critics who denounce them.

The descendants of Fat-Cheeks's followers preserved the Authorized Version of our story. Over millennia they evolved a snake-handling ceremony to drive the message home. Each year, at the spring equinox, the Alpha male, whose royal or institutional name was Fat-Cheeks, handled a black mamba that a flunky had secretly defanged. Following the ceremony, everyone got a piece of black mamba to eat, like it or not. Millennia still later, they evolved a substitute for the snake, a hobby snake, a *stake* in fact, for over millennia the repressed slowly returns—or did I say that? By now the People of Fat-Cheeks had killed off the big game around their ancestral home, so they too moved to the Near East, which was getting nearer. There they quickly conquered the descendants of the People who had gone into exile with Short-Shanks. The victors continued to call themselves "The People," but they called their victims "The Others," so as to signify that they were fair game. For the sake of convenience we will follow this nomenclature, if it is understood that my doing so implies no valorization of either party. The People, then, pressed the Others into service as slaves and serfs, for being warriors and hunters, they considered farming beneath them. But being also shrewd, like their culture hero, they recruited promising young Others for the lower clerisy.

One unemployed young Other, who had been trained as a scribe, refused the role of flunky. Besides, no one would hire him. He was untidy, gaunt, eloquent, and sexually ambiguous. Millennia before, he would have been a berdache or shaman, except that no matter how hard he tried, he just couldn't bring on a vision. He tried hacking off a finger, starving in the desert, eating forbidden mushrooms, but the vision never came. Finally, in desperation, he sought out the last of the sorcerers, a blind ancient who lived in scrofulous poverty and in a batty cave. The young man stood before the sorcerer and spoke these words: "What is to be done?" The sorcerer, who was senile, mumbled his answer: "Fat-Cheeks hefted a snake," by which he seems to have meant, "Go find a job." But the young man fell in a fit and thrashed around for a while in the bat guano. When he woke up, he began to preach, for he had at last had his vision.

He traveled among the flotsam of the city and the jetsam of the countryside, calling himself Son of Others, spreading the good news. For his vision had revealed to him how in the beginning the Great Goddess danced in the void. She called herself Fat-Cheeks because, like many dancers, she was both steato- and calli-pygous. Her pirouettes created a whirlwind, which she rolled out between her hands until it was very like a snake. When it reared up with forked tongue, bared fangs, and a blood-curdling hiss, she mounted it. From this union came all things, including the Others, whom the Goddess chose for her own. Under Her mild sway, the Others at first lived in a pastoral paradise of polymorphous perversity—until they were conquered by the People, who bowed down to male demons, ate meat, and were otherwise disgusting. Their Alpha male had usurped the Goddess's name and prerogatives, had expropriated the sacred black mamba, symbol of Her power and instrument of Her bounty. But now Son of Others had been elected to prepare the way for Her return. The Days of Wrath were upon us. Soon She would ride in on a whirlwind. She would blow the People away and restore the Others to their pastoral paradise. This gospel spread like wildfire. Disciples swelled the ranks and purged deviationists. And so it was that "Fat-Cheeks hefted a snake" became the world's first revolutionary slogan.

For in their way with literature, anti-institutional institutions are like the other kind.

There is no need for me to go on with how Son of Others and the Others took charge; how they began to call themselves "the People" and to call other people "the Others"; how in the fertile valleys of the Meander they established the world's first oriental despotism, thus bringing the Near East still nearer; how cadres of untidy heretics met secretly to expound the true gospel, which told how Fat-Cheeks, Father of all things, puffed out his face like a black mamba to blow life into the first clay men, ancestors of the Others, whom He chose for his own. I have already said enough to illustrate my point, which has nine parts: 1. Literature doesn't exist. 2. It is an institution. 3. It is anti-institutional in origin. 4. It is a substitute. 5. That is its institutional function. 6. The institutional function of critics is to convert it to other institutional functions. 7. The disposition of individuals is to deinstitutionalize it. 8. The disposition of anti-institutional institutions is to reinstitutionalize it. 9. Thus literature survives by adapting itself to intraspecific pressures.

I don't suppose I can get out of declaring myself on the question as to whether or not the institutionalization of literature is a good thing. I could evade the issue for a moment by observing that it is as inevitable as aging: if you live, you get old; if literature lives, it gets institutionalized. But you don't have to like something just because it's inevitable. All right, here goes: my answer to the question of whether or not the institutionalization of literature is a good thing . . . depends—it depends on which I value more, literature or institutions; and that depends on which literature and which institutions are in question; it depends on whether or not the institutions in question are adaptive. Suppose I leave it for you to decide whether or not our literary institutions are adaptive. I have already hefted more than one snake too many.

The English Institute, 1979

The Program

Friday, August 31, through Monday, September 3, 1979

I. English as a World Language for Literature
    Directed by Houston A. Baker, Jr., University of Pennsylvania

       Fri. 1:45 P.M.   English and the Dynamics of South African Creative Writing
    Dennis Brutus, Northwestern University

       Sat. 9:30 A.M.   English in the Caribbean: Notes on the Writing Process
    Edward Brathwaite, University of the West Indies

       Sat. 11:00 A.M.   Native American Literature and the Uses of English
    Leslie Silko, University of New Mexico

II. George Eliot
    Directed by Felicia Bonaparte, City University of New York

       Fri. 3:15 P.M.   From Mary Shelley to George Eliot: The Non-Anxieties of Uninfluence
    U. C. Knoepflmacher, Princeton University and the University of California, Berkeley

       Sat. 1:45 P.M.   George Eliot's Scientific Ideal: The Hypothesis of Reality
    George Levine, Rutgers University

       Sat. 3:15 P.M.   George Eliot's Next Novel: An Exercise in Constructionist Fictional Criticism
    Jerome Beaty, Emory University

III. Allegory
    Directed by Paul De Man, Yale University

       Sun. 9:30 A.M.   The Structure of Allegorical Desire
    Joel Fineman, University of California, Berkeley

       Sun. 11:00 A.M.   Deceit and Digestion in Dante's Hell
    Robert Durling, University of California, Santa Cruz

       Mon. 9:30 A.M.   Florio's Montaigne
    Tom Clark Conley, University of Minnesota

155

Mon. 11:00 A.M.   Pascal's Allegory of Persuasion
                  Paul De Man, Yale University

IV. The Institution of Literature
   Directed by Leslie Fiedler, State University of New York, Buffalo
       Sun. 1:45 P.M.   English as an Institution: the Role of Class
                           Bruce Franklin, Rutgers University
       Sun. 3:15 P.M.   English as an Institution: the Role of Sex
                           Diana George, Pennsylvania State University,
                           The Behrend College
       Mon. 1:45 P.M.   English as an Institution: Popular Culture
                           George Stade, Columbia University
       Mon. 3:15 P.M.   English as an Institution: an Overview
                           Leslie Fiedler, State University of New York,
                           Buffalo

Sponsoring Institutions

Columbia University, Princeton University, Yale University, University of Rochester, Claremont Graduate School, Rutgers University, Michigan State University, Northwestern University, Boston University, University of California at Berkeley, University of Connecticut, Harvard University, University of Pennsylvania, University of Virginia, Amherst College, State University of New York at Stony Brook, City University of New York Graduate Center, Brandeis University, Cornell University, Dartmouth College, New York University, Smith College, The Johns Hopkins University, Washington University, State University of New York at Albany, Temple University, University of Alabama at Birmingham, University of California at San Diego, Boston College, Brigham Young University, University of California at Los Angeles, University of California at Santa Cruz, Massachusetts Institute of Technology, Wellesley College, Indiana University at Bloomington, Stanford University.

Registrants, 1979

Ruth M. Adams, Dartmouth College; Joseph Adams, SUNY-Binghamton; Samuel W. Allen, Boston University; Valborg Anderson, Brooklyn College, CUNY; Jonathan Arac, University of Illinois at Chicago Circle; N. S. Asbridge, Central Connecticut State College

Houston A. Baker, Jr., University of Pennsylvania; Frank Baldanza, Bowling Green State University; Evelyn Barish, College of Staten Island, CUNY; Bertrice Bartlett, Stephens College; Jerome Beaty, Emory University; John E. Becker, Fairleigh Dickinson University; Millicent Bell, Boston University; Alice R. Bensen, Eastern Michigan University; Bernard & Shari Benstock, University of Illinois; Carole Berger, Dartmouth College; John B. Beston, Kuwait University; Jean Frantz Blackall, Cornell University; Morton W. Bloomfield, Harvard; Charles R. Blyth; Felicia Bonaparte, City University of New York; Marie Borroff, Yale University; Carol Bové, Franklin School; Paul A. Bové, University of Pittsburgh; Francis R. Bowers, FSC, Manhattan College; John D. Boyd, S.J., Fordham University; Frank Brady, CUNY Graduate Center; Edward Kamau Brathwaite, University of the West Indies; Laurence A. Breiner, Boston University; Dr.

Olga R. R. Broomfield, Mount Saint Vincent University; Marianne Broch, Mount Holyoke College; Julia Brown, Boston University; Dennis Brutus, Northwestern University; Jane Britton Buchanan, Tufts University; Willis R. Buck, Jr., Temple University; Daniel Burke, F.S.L., La Salle College; Andrew Busza, University of British Columbia; Mervin Butovsky, Concordia University

Janice Carlisle, University of Virgina; Robert L. Caserio, Yale University; Elaine Campbell, Brandeis University; M. Kent Casper, University of Colorado; Arnold H. Chadderdon, Whittier College; Lila Chalpin, Mass. College; Priscilla P. Clark, University of Illinois; Arlene L. Clift, Fisk University; Arthur N. Collins, State University of New York at Albany; Tom Clark Conley, University of Minnesota; Bainard Cowan, Louisiana State University; Patricia Craddock, Boston University; G. Armour Craig, Amherst College; Stuart Curran, University of Pennsylvania; William M. Curtin, University of Connecticut

Peter Dale, Harvard University; Emily Dalgarno, Boston University; Elizabeth Adams Daniels, Vassar College; Tom Dargan; Winifred M. Davis, Columbia University; Robert A. Day, Queens College, CUNY; Paul De Man, Yale University; Evelyn C. Dodge, Framingham State College; Charlotte F. Domke, Johnson State College; George W. Domke, Johnson State College; E. T. Donaldson, Indiana University; Sister Rose Bernard Donna, The College of Saint Rose; Robert Durling, University of California, Santa Cruz

Robert C. Elliott, University of California; David A. Ellis, Boston University; John M. Ellis, University of California; W. R. Elton, Graduate School, City University of New York; Martha W. England, Queens College; David V. Erdman, State University of New York; Elizabeth Ermarth, University of Maryland

N. N. Feltes, York University; Earl Fendelman, Herbert H. Lehman College; Anne Lathrop Fessenden, Seton Hall University; Leslie Fiedler, State University of New York; Joel Fineman, University of California; Leslie D. Foster, Northern Michigan University; Bruce Franklin, Rutgers–Newark; Warren G. French, Indiana University; Michael Fried, The Johns Hopkins University; Albert B. Friedman, Claremont Graduate School; Michael H. Friedman; W. M. Frohock, Harvard; Everett C. Frost; Margaretta Fulton, Harvard University Press; John M. Fyler, Tufts University

Robert E. Garlitz, Plymouth State College; Harry R. Garvin, Bucknell

University; Edward A. Geary, Brigham Young University; Blanche H. Gelfant, Dartmouth College; Charisse Gendron, University of Connecticut; Diana Hume George, Pennsylvania State University, The Behrend College; Arthur Gold, Wellesley College; Linda S. Goldberg, Northeastern University; George Goodin, Southern Illinois University; Linda Silverstein Gordon, Boston State College; Harry Girling, York University; Terry H. Grabar, Fitchburg State College; Suzanne Graver, Williams College; James Gray, Dalhousie University; Stephen Greenblatt, University of California; Michael Groden, University of Western Ontario; Laila Z. Gross, Bunting Institute

David P. Haney, Boston College; George M. Hanold, Bard College; Barbara Leah Harman, Wellesley College; Richard Harrier, New York University; Mason Harris, Simon Fraser University; Victor Harris, Brandeis University; Edward L. Hart, Brigham Young University; Phillip Harth, University of Wisconsin; Geoffrey Hartman, Yale University; Joan E. Hartman, College of Staten Island, CUNY; Nahla Zuhdi Hashweh, University of Virginia; Richard Haven, University of Massachusetts; Michael Hays, Columbia University; Patrick D. Hazard, Beaver College; Suzette Henke, SUNY Binghamton; Bruce Herzberg, Clark University; Margaret R. Higonnet, University of Connecticut; Barbara Ann Hill, Hood College; John M. Hill, U.S. Naval Academy; William B. Hill, S.J., University of Scranton; Daniel Hoffman, University of Pennsylvania; C. Fenno Hoffman, Jr., Rhode Island School; Laurence B. Holland, The Johns Hopkins University; Julia Bolton Holloway, Princeton University; Margaret Homans, Yale University; Vivian C. Hopkins, State University of New York; Kay S. House, San Francisco State University; Virginia R. Hyman, Newark College, Rutgers University; Lawrence W. Hyman, Brooklyn College

Nora Crow Jaffe, Smith College; Abdul R. JanMohamed, Boston University; Kenneth Johnston, Indiana University; Iva G. Jones, Morgan State University; Sidney C. Jones, Carroll College; John E. Jordan, University of California; Gerhard Joseph, Herbert H. Lehman College, CUNY; Lee Jung-Kee, Yale University

Arthur F. Kinney, University of Massachusetts; Karl Kiralis, California State; Rudolf Kirk, Rutgers University; U. C. Knoepflmacher, Princeton University; Theodora J. Koob, Shippensburg State College; Andrea F. Korval, Brooklyn College; Lawrence Kramer, Fordham University

Gerard P. Lair, Delbarton School; Roy Lamson, Massachusetts Institute;

Berel Lang, University of Colorado; Nancy Leonard, Bard College; Vivien Leonard, Rensselear Polytechnic Institute; George Levine, Livingston College, Rutgers University; Dwight N. Lindley, Hamilton College; Katherine Bailey Linehan, Oberlin College; Susan E. Linville, Massachusetts Institute; James T. Livingston, Drury College; Joseph P. Lovering, Canisius College; Sister Alice Lubin, Saint Elizabeth College; Daniel P. Luker, Delbarton School

Warren J. MacIsaac, Catholic University; Arthur F. Marotti, Wayne State University; Howard A. Mayer, University of Connecticut; Terence J. McKenzie, U.S. Coast Guard Academy; Donald C. Mell, Jr., University of Delaware; Dorothy Mermin, Cornell University; Dorthee Metlitzki, Yale University; Jay Ronald Meyers, East Stroudsburg State College; Alan L. Mintz, Columbia University; Goldstein Mulum, University of Hartford

John M. Nesselhof, Wells College; Clare H. Nunes; Margaret Neussendorfer, Radcliffe College

Martha A. O'Brien, Dublin College; Richard Ohmann, Wesleyan University; Richard Onorato, Brandeis University; Charles Owen, University of Connecticut

Stanley R. Palombo, Washington School of Psychiatry; Julia Distefano Pappageorge, SUNY Stony Brook; James G. Paradis, Massachusetts Institute; Stephen M. Parrish, Cornell University; Coleman O. Parsons, University of New York; Emily H. Patterson, San Diego State University; Felix L. Paul, West Virginia State College; Ronald Paulson, Yale University; Roy Harvey Pearce, University of California; Justus R. Pearson, Jr., Illinois Wesleyan University; Nancy Pell, University of New York; Ruth Perlmutter, Philadelphia College; Linda Peterson, Yale University; Richard S. Peterson, Yale University; Richard Poirier, Rutgers University; David Porter, University of Massachusetts; Thomas Postlewait, Massachusetts Institute; Robert O. Preyer, Brandeis University; John W. Price, Middlesex School

Joan Reardon, Barat College; Gail T. Reimer, Rutgers University; Neale Reinitz, Colorado College; James Richardson, Harvard University; James Rieger, University of Rochester; Harriet Ritvo, Massachusetts Institute; Bruce Robbins, University of Geneva; Jeffrey C. Robinson, University of Colorado; John Romano, Columbia University; Sergio Rossi, Università Di Torino–Italy

Elaine B. Safer, University of Delaware; Edward W. Said, Columbia University; Nancy and Thomas N. Salter, Eastern Connecticut State College; Dianella Savoia, University of Padva; Zulema Seligsohn, Hunter College-CUNY; Joseph L. Schneider and Waltraud Schneider-Mitgutsch, Seoul National University and Ewha Women's University; Samuel Schulman, Boston University; H. T. Schultz, Dartmouth College; Susan Field Senneff, Columbia University; R. A. Shoaf, Yale University; Elaine Showalter, Douglas College; Heather Rosarid Sievert, New York University; William Sievert, Pace University; Leslie Marmon Silko, University of New Mexico; Patricia L. Skarda, Smith College; Alexander Smith, Jr., University of Connecticut; Barbara Herrnstein Smith, University of Pennsylvania; Sarah W. R. Smith, Tufts University; Thomas N. Smith, University of Hartford; Patricia Meyer Spacks, Yale University; Jeffrey L. Spear, Princeton University; Sheila A. Spector; Robert Spiller, University of Pennsylvania; Robert Sprich, Bentley College; George Stade, Columbia University; J. D. Stahl, University of Connecticut; Rhoda M. Staley, State University of New York; Richard Stamelman, Wesleyan University; Susan Staves, Brandeis; Robert A. Stein, University of Lowell; Robert Sternbach, Boston University; Holly Stevens; Fred E. Stockholder, University of British Columbia; Albert Stone, Jr., Hellenic College; Gary Lee Stonum, Case Western Reserve; Rudolf F. Storch, Tufts University; Maureen Sullivan, Marquette University; Stanley Sultan, Clark University; Deborah Swedberg, Boston University

Anne Robinson Taylor, Oregon State University; Irene Tayler, Massachusetts Institute; Elizabeth Tenenbaum, State University of New York; David Thorburn, Massachusetts Institute; Elza Tiner, University of Toronto; Rosemary Barton Tobin, Emmannel College; J. J. M. Tobin, Boston State College; C. James Trotman, West Chester State College; Ralph Tutt, University of Rhode Island

Helen Vendler, Boston University

Melissa G. Walker, Mercer University; Eugene M. Waith, Yale University; Aileen Ward, Brandeis University; M. Charlotte Ward, University of Connecticut; Helen A. Weinberg, Cleveland Institute; Richard H. Weisberg, Cardozo Law School; Hayden White, University of California; Epi Wiese; Joseph Wiesenfarth, University of Wisconsin; Wilburn Williams; Massachusetts Institute; Judith Wilt, Boston College; Joseph A. Witterich, Jr.; Cynthia Griffin Wolff, University of Massachusetts; Michael Wolff, University of Massachusetts; Mildred Worthington

Rose Zak, Boston College